HOUSING REFORM DURING
THE TRUMAN ADMINISTRATION

Housing Reform

During the

Truman Administration

by

RICHARD O. DAVIES

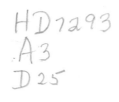
UNIVERSITY OF MISSOURI PRESS

Columbia, Missouri

Publication of this book
has been aided by the Ford Foundation program
to support publication,
through university presses, of work in the
humanities and social sciences

"A decent standard of housing for all is one of the irreducible obligations of modern civilization."

—Harry S Truman
Message to Congress, September 6, 1945

Acknowledgments

MANY PERSONS contributed significantly to this study. I am especially grateful for the patient and perceptive guidance of Professor Richard S. Kirkendall of the University of Missouri. He instilled in me a deep interest in the history of the Truman era and gave freely of his time during the research and writing of an earlier version of this study, which served as my doctoral dissertation. I benefited also from the suggestions of Professor Allen F. Davis of the University of Missouri, Columbia, Professor Lyle W. Dorsett of the University of Missouri at St. Louis, and Professor Frank D. Mitchell of Washburn University. I naturally assume full responsibility for possible error of fact or interpretation.

Much of the research was supported by a grant from The Harry S. Truman Library Institute. Dr. Philip C. Brooks and his staff at The Harry S. Truman Library made an extended research visit in Independence a profitable and pleasant experience. Mr. Hilbert Fefferman of the Housing and Home Finance Agency made available important materials still in the possession of the agency, and Professor J. Joseph Huthmacher of Georgetown University facilitated research in the papers of Senator Robert F. Wagner. Mrs. Jeri Guthrie typed the final manuscript, and Mr. William Brunemeyer provided invaluable editorial assistance. Throughout the several years devoted to this project, my wife Sharon has been the cheerful source of encouragement and of patient understanding. I also wish to acknowledge the continued encouragement and wise counsel provided by my parents, Mr. and Mrs. Robert O. Davies, without whose help I would never have begun this study.

R.O.D.

Northern Arizona University
Flagstaff, Arizona

Introduction

Mr. Blandings Builds His Dream House

S OCIAL and economic reform has provided a basic ingredient of twentieth-century American political history. The emergence of an urban and industrial society forced American liberalism to reject *laissez faire* in favor of the pragmatism of the regulatory and social service functions of progressivism and the New Deal. The reforms of Theodore Roosevelt, Woodrow Wilson, and, especially, Franklin D. Roosevelt altered century-old concepts about the relationship between the individual citizen and his government. Grover Cleveland's belief that a person should support his government but not expect anything in return was displaced by the new truths of social security and a minimum wage.

It was this social service function of government that President Harry S Truman attempted to perpetuate and expand. Throughout his years in the White House, the doughty Missourian fought for legislative reforms he believed would give most Americans a "fair deal." In spite of herculean efforts, his reform accomplishments were minimal. Balky

Congresses—both Democratic and Republican—rejected his pleas for basic legislation in the areas of civil rights, medical care, and education. The Brannan Plan for agriculture was defeated, and the Taft-Hartley Act was passed over his veto. For the achievement of domestic reforms no President has worked harder and accomplished less. If Truman is to be awarded the mantle of "great" for his actions during his tenure as President, it will have to be for his conduct of foreign policy.

But lack of reform legislation does not detract from the historical significance of the Truman Administration. Although he added little to the accomplishments of the previous fifty years, he prevented the emasculation of those reforms by a hostile Congress. Just as he attempted to contain Communist expansion in foreign policy, Truman sought to preserve the reforms of the New Deal in his domestic policy.[1] Even the major Fair Deal legislative triumph—the Housing Act of 1949—merely revised and expanded a New Deal program.

This study focuses upon the housing policies of the Fair Deal and is based upon the assumptions that they contributed significantly to the politics of the Truman Administration and that housing reform is, in itself, an important part of twentieth-century American history. But as the narrative indicates, no single reform can be isolated from the entire spectrum of activity that occurred between 1945 and 1953.

The many housing programs that Truman attempted to establish or continue were, primarily, pragmatic responses to a critical political situation; but each was also deeply rooted in the previous fifty years of urban-oriented reform that had originated with a few social workers and reformers during the progressive era and had come to fruition during the New Deal. Such Truman-supported programs as slum clearance, public housing, expansion of Federal Housing Administration mortgage insurance, federal loans to middle-income housing cooperatives, rent controls, and an emergency program for veterans' housing shared not only the heritage of progressivism but also a newly adopted goal: decent housing for every American family.

Truman's approach to housing policy and especially to the politically important program of public housing was based upon the progressive assumption that decent housing is a basic factor in the creation of a strong democratic society. Good housing is not simply clean rooms and an indoor bathroom; it is also a creator of fundamental attitudes and therefore a factor in social regeneration. Housing reformers during the Truman Administration emphasized that poor housing *creates* much of the social disorder associated with urban slums. Poor housing, they argued, is the major cause of high rates of crime, vice, mental illness, juvenile delinquency, and divorce. Decent public housing for low-income families decreases these problems and could, ultimately, eradicate them. To the dedicated housing reformer of the time, public housing was not just a humanitarian program designed to alleviate the miseries of urban poverty; it was the panacea that would elevate the aspirations of the residents and inculcate in them the basic ideals of democracy. More important, it would transform them into industrious and useful citizens. Fair Deal housing reform, therefore, was directly linked to the moralistic assumptions of progressivism and to the naïve optimism that pervaded much of that earlier reform movement. It was the Truman Administration's unquestioning acceptance of the social uplift argument that was to cause, ultimately, the failure of this single, most important Truman housing policy.

But circumstances in the early days of Truman's Presidency, during which the housing policies were formulated, precluded a deliberate and analytical approach to housing policy because a pressing national housing shortage created a political crisis that demanded immediate solution. With the return of the veterans following V-J Day, a shortage of moderately priced houses and rental apartments made housing a major political issue. This was the time when Mr. Blandings built his dream house, and the sales success of this popular novel reflected widespread interest in housing.[2] Whether the dream house was a privately built split-level or a federally financed low-rent, achieving the dream was a pressing matter for most Americans, as Harry S Truman led the nation into the uncertainties of the postwar years.

The national interest in housing had begun to grow shortly after Pearl Harbor. Even during the unhappy war year of 1942, the idea that every American should have a decent home of his own began to percolate in the minds of servicemen and civilians alike. By 1945, improved housing had become a national objective, and Franklin D. Roosevelt, always aware of the new tendencies in public opinion, announced that one of his major postwar goals was adequate housing for all Americans. This interest, however, was not a mere wartime craze, but a manifestation of a deeply rooted part of the American Dream. The Lockean ideal of private property, firmly entrenched in the American mind during the Colonial period and sanctified by the agrarianism of Thomas Jefferson, had slowly been transformed through urbanization and industrialism into the nearly sacred institution of the American home. The triphammer shocks of the Great Depression and the Second World War had revived and strengthened this deeply ingrained desire for home ownership. The wholesale mortgage foreclosures, the Hoovervilles, and the general feeling of helplessness during the thirties made Americans more determined than ever to own their own homes. In a perceptive analysis of the American mind during the bleak days of his Administration, Herbert Hoover had observed:

> I am confident that the sentiment for home ownership is so embedded in the American heart that millions of people who dwell in tenements, apartments, and rental rows of solid brick have the aspiration for wider opportunity in ownership of their own home.[3]

As house construction dwindled to the century's low point

in 1933 and the percentage of rentals steadily rose, the ideal of home ownership became increasingly more important. By 1940, however, as the depression caused the tenancy rate to soar to an all-time high, this ideal seemed to be merely an elusive mirage. The war acted as a catalyst upon this latent feeling and produced a widespread, conscious interest in postwar housing. As 13,000,000 men risked death in war, many Americans sought a proper reward for "G.I. Joe." To many, providing the opportunity to enjoy the security and satisfaction of home ownership seemed to be an excellent means of expressing the nation's gratitude.[4] This altruism was abetted by wartime prosperity, which helped lift individual goals as full employment and overtime pay swelled bank accounts and rationing and scarcities blocked the usual avenues of expenditure. The desire for better housing, feeding upon the frustrations and heartbreaks of the depression and the horrors of war, burgeoned among Americans. For many, this meant buying a new home; for others, renting a larger apartment; and for some, simply occupying a clean flat with modern plumbing. The demand for better housing, pent up by the war, burst forth with the announcement of the Japanese surrender and caused an unprecedented housing shortage that lasted until the early 1950's. This enthusiasm for better housing provided for those persons concerned with housing reform a generally accepted motive that they could mold into a concerted drive for large government housing programs. Housing reformers shrewdly fused the general public's interest with their own goals of greatly expanded public housing and slum clearance programs to produce a powerful political movement that demanded the elimination of all slum housing in the United States.

Because of the extensive national interest in better housing, the activism of reformers, and, especially, the critical postwar housing shortage, housing policy played an important role in Fair Deal politics. President Harry S Truman devoted considerable attention to this issue and made "a decent house in a good environment for every American family" one of his major reform objectives. His failure to accomplish this worthy goal resulted from many factors, including resourceful political opposition from real estate groups and entrenched rural congressional leaders, but, most important, from the acceptance of the progressive assumption that poor housing is the cause, and not the result, of other social disorders.

Contents

Chapter I

The Foundations of a Housing Program

THE CONTINUED growth of urban areas has been one of the most important developments in twentieth-century American history. The emergence of the large city has contributed much to the composition of modern society, and it in turn has transformed the rural areas in its own image and imposed its values and culture upon all Americans.[1] In most rural areas in the United States, Americans read urban newspapers, watch television, and listen to radio programs. The average farm housewife shops at a supermarket, casts her wardrobe according to the latest fashion magazines, and looks forward to her semiannual trip to the city for the purchase of a new refrigerator or living room suite. Even the "country bumpkin" is almost extinct; on the sidewalks of Chicago or Kansas City, the farm dweller is indistinguishable from the urbanite.

The city has also placed its indelible stamp on national politics, which only slowly and reluctantly responded to the continued growth of the urban areas. As the urban population surpassed that of the farm, a political revolution occurred. The cities, becoming increasingly Democratic, turned the proud and nearly invincible Republican party of 1900 into a defeated minority party by 1940. The Democratic urban coalition began to take shape during the 1920's under the leadership of Alfred E. Smith, but because of the Republicans' strength outside the big cities, this change in political alignment went unnoticed. By 1932 the urban-Democratic vote had outstripped the rural-Republican, but the nationwide revulsion against Herbert Hoover concealed this political revolution, just as Franklin D. Roosevelt's great popularity did in 1936. In his first two Presidential campaigns Roosevelt would have won without the large urban majorities he received, but in 1940 and 1944, when rural voters returned to their old alignments, the city vote was essential to Democratic success. In fact, ten urban states were the decisive factor in Roosevelt's victory; without their support the Republicans would have returned to power.[2] Consequently, Roosevelt responded to the reform demands of the urban coalition, since it now held the key to future Democratic success.

These reforms represented the wishes of the hard core of the Roosevelt coalition, which was composed primarily of labor, low-income, and minority groups. This new reform movement, aptly named "urban liberalism," added a new dimension to American reform.[3] It discarded the traditional American ideals of self-reliance and individual initiative as inapplicable to an urban-industrial society and espoused in their place government regulation and welfare programs as the only means of protecting the urban lower classes. During the progressive period, urban liberalism fought for such programs as tenement inspection, workmen's compensation, and factory safety laws, and during the New Deal it secured the passage of the Social Security Act, the Fair Labor Standards Act, the National Industrial Recovery Act, the National Labor Relations Act, and the United States Housing Act. Urban liberalism rejected nineteenth-century liberalism and viewed government as an instrument of positive action to protect and aid the working classes. It gained strength with the expanding urban population and closely aligned itself with the national Democratic party.[4] By 1940 urban liberalism constituted the major reform impulse in the nation and had succeeded in turning the once radical and reformist midwestern and southern agricultural areas into centers of conservative opposition to this new brand of reform.[5]

One of the important programs of urban liberalism was improved housing for all income groups. The history of housing reform in the twentieth century corresponds closely with the development of urban liberalism. Although the first known effort to deal with slum housing occurred in New York City in 1834, reform attempts were sporadic and ineffectual until after 1900. Throughout the nineteenth century, housing reformers were primarily charity workers who operated within the framework of the prevalent ideas of individual responsibility and paternalism. Believing that poverty is a result of individual weakness, most of the reformers directed their efforts toward teaching slum dwellers the virtues of thrift, self-reliance, and morality. Apparently, it was assumed that the only way to end slum housing was to instruct tenement dwellers how to improve their characters.[6]

By the turn of the century, however, a new form of housing reform emerged which realized that *laissez faire* and Christian paternalism would not solve the problem of low-income housing. Housing reformers now turned hopefully, although timidly, toward government regulation. Most of these reformers were social workers who came from substantial middle- and upper-class families. When they entered the urban low-income districts, the poor housing conditions immediately engaged their attention. In many respects, the various reform efforts of the social justice movement stemmed from the desire to improve urban living conditions. Throughout the twentieth century social workers have provided the hard core of the drive for housing reform.[7]

Prior to 1917 all reform attempts were regulatory in nature, that is, they were devised to maintain minimum standards of housing. Reform had not yet advanced to the position of government housing, and the aversion to minimum standards legislation was still great, even among housing reformers. Most reformers disliked the need for such action, but they could find no acceptable alternative and therefore advocated inspection laws as the only logical solution.

Although there had been previous tenement laws, the first effective one was the New York Tenement Inspection Law of 1901, which provided for minimum health standards and established the Tenement House Commission to enforce the law. Largely the product of Jacob Riis's journalistic efforts, this law served as a model for all cities wishing to enact their own inspection laws. Although the reformers did not directly challenge the position of the tenement owners, housing was now considered within the scope of government regulation. In 1903 Lawrence Veiller, secretary of the New York Tenement Commission, and Robert De Forest, a corporation lawyer who had become a reformer, published *The Tenement House Problem*, in which they clearly documented the evils of slum housing and proposed solutions to the problem. Paul Kellogg's *Pittsburgh Survey*, a seven-volume work, presented a microscopic study of the need for urban reform. These works served as guides for reformers until the First World War. In 1911 reformers organized the National Housing Association to help promote nationwide reform.[8]

After 1900 housing reform grew in size and scope as city planners, architects, land economists, city officials, public health officers, journalists, and political leaders joined the movement. City planners, imbued with the ideas of Frederick Law Olmstead and Ebenezer Howard, added a new dimension to the movement as they advocated greenbelts within the cities and even construction of completely new garden cities.

Architects found in row houses a possible alternative to tenement housing.[9] Social workers believed housing reform to be the key to the elimination of the major urban social problems of delinquency, immorality, and disease, while politicians looked upon it as a means to obtain the support of voters in the tenement districts. Few, however, were ready to move beyond the enforcement of minimum standards or the erection of private "limited dividend" housing projects. Just as Veiller, father of housing reform, decried government-subsidized public housing in 1902, on the ground that it would "undermine our ancestral habit of self-reliance," the National Housing Association convention in 1916 cheered a speaker who said he did not believe that the time would ever arrive when American taxpayers would be willing to allow government housing to be built for the benefit of the poor.[10]

A national crisis, however, often changes firmly established ideas. When a critical housing shortage for defense workers developed during World War I, the federal government, spurning dogma, built the necessary housing. Operating through the United States Shipping Board's Emergency Fleet Corporation and the Department of Labor's United States Housing Corporation, the government built and maintained 15,183 family units and 14,745 single units in twenty-four eastern shipbuilding locations. Although the government sold the projects immediately after the war, this program demonstrated the possibilities of government housing in the United States and gave reformers a practical example of public housing for low-income families.[11]

During the 1920's public housing was generally unacceptable, and reformers contented themselves with improving inspection laws and building experimental housing developments financed by private investors. Under the guidance of the Regional Planning Association and the Russell Sage Foundation, reformers constructed two garden cities: Radburn, New Jersey, and Sunnyside, on Long Island. Although such communities attracted considerable attention, they held no real solution to the problem of providing adequate housing for millions of low-income families. A small but influential group of social workers, led by Helen Alfred and Mary Simkhovitch, sponsored a movement to provide acceptable housing for low-income families. These dedicated persons, without the aid of the publicity that surrounded the planned communities, held many conferences and continued to make detailed studies of urban housing conditions. The results of these studies, they held, showed that most of the urban social problems originated with poor housing. Eliminate the slums, they argued, and immorality, disease, delinquency, and other related disorders would be drastically reduced. By 1930 many of the social workers realized that the maintenance of minimum standards by the use of inspection laws was a failure, so they turned to government-subsidized public housing as the only logical alternative solution. Although housing reformers actually accomplished little during the twenties, they succeeded in keeping the movement alive and, by investigating the proposed programs, prepared themselves for the exciting years of the New Deal.[12]

The Great Depression severely crippled the national economy and provided an atmosphere in which experiment and new ideas were readily received by the public. Between 1931 and 1937 more significant developments in housing reform occurred than in the previous one hundred years. Continued questioning of the exact role of the private housing industry in the American economy underlay the flurry of housing reform activity. Although most reformers constantly reaffirmed their faith in the potentialities of private housing, the federal government assumed many new responsibilities in the housing field. Most of the programs were designed to aid private housing directly, but despite such help, private housing still could not adequately serve low-income families. Following the leadership of the social workers, who had carefully developed a workable federal public housing program during the 1920's, the political leaders slowly accepted public housing as the best means of attacking the long-enduring problem of low-income housing.[13]

The Hoover Administration had attempted to pump new life into the stagnant home-building industry in 1931 by calling the President's Conference on Home Building and Home Ownership. The major result of this conference, in which 3,700 persons participated, was the creation of the Federal Home Loan Bank Board, which established twelve district Federal Home Loan banks to maintain a reserve credit organization for home-financing institutions. This program attempted to provide a wider and better distribution of the funds available for home financing. One of the many reports filed by the conference called for public housing, and it received Hoover's endorsement along with the other reports. The Hoover Administration, in a major break with tradition, authorized the Reconstruction Finance Corporation to make loans to corporations formed to build low-cost housing; this program, however, proved ineffectual, as only one project was constructed.[14]

The New Deal drastically enlarged the government's role in housing. Just as the emergency of the First World War produced a brief flirtation with public housing, the great shock caused by the collapse of the economy led to a flurry of government housing activity. As in other areas where government activity had been minimal or nonexistent, the federal government now became an active participant. Before the end of this intensified welfare and reform movement, the federal government had entered into most areas of housing. The primary purpose of all of the programs was to revive the badly depressed housing industry through rejuvenation of the lending institutions and the construction business; reform was only a secondary aim. In 1933 Congress established the Home Owners' Loan Corporation under the Federal Home Loan Bank Board for the purpose of aiding home owners faced with mortgage foreclosures. The HOLC eventually refinanced over one million mortgages by offering long-term loans at 5 per cent interest. To restore public confidence in savings and loan companies, the National Housing Act of 1934 established the Federal Savings and Loan Insurance Corporation to insure savings up to $5,000 in the participating institutions. This act also created the Federal Housing Administration, the purpose of which was to insure individual home mortgages. FHA's underwriting system attempted to standardize home mortgage lending practices and improve housing standards.[15]

The federal government became directly involved also in the construction of houses. Under the legislative generalship of Senator Robert F. Wagner (Dem., N.Y.), low-cost housing was included in the public works section of the National Industrial Recovery Act. Under the bill, a total of 21,769 public housing units were built. The program's scope was quite limited because of legal snarls, local apathy, and the slowness of PWA's watchdog, Harold Ickes, to approve proposed projects.[16] In 1935 the Resettlement Administration, under Rexford G. Tugwell, began construction of three "greenbelt" garden cities; these communities, patterned after Radburn and Sunnyside, proved to be only an interesting experiment, as the widespread criticism they engendered prevented the erection of other such communities.[17]

The final New Deal housing program proved to be the most significant. In 1937 Congress passed the United States Housing Act, which contained a large public housing program. A small but determined group of housing reformers, led by Mrs. Mary Simkhovitch, helped Wagner prod Congress into passing the bill. Although Roosevelt spoke eloquently in behalf of "one-third of a nation ill housed" in his 1937 inaugural address,[18] he did little to help the passage of the bill. Timothy McDonnell, in his detailed study of the bill's passage, points out that Roosevelt had little interest in housing reform; in fact, the bill could have become law one year earlier had Roosevelt supported it. This he refused to do, and the bill died in committee. When Congress finally passed the bill in 1937, the action was due, not to any effort by Roosevelt, but to Wagner's forceful leadership and the concerted efforts of urban pressure groups and social reformers.[19] This bill, a milestone in housing reform, actually passed Congress as primarily an economic stimulant, not as a reform measure. The most effective argument used by the bill's supporters was that it would help revive the stagnant housing industry; housing reform would be a pleasant byproduct.[20] Under the Wagner Housing Act the United States Housing Authority eventually provided funds for local housing authorities to build 117,755 units of public housing in the place of razed slums.[21] This act linked slum clearance and public housing under one program. Under the "equivalent elimination" provision of the law at least one unit of public housing had to be constructed to replace each leveled slum dwelling unit.[22] This restrictive feature was removed by the Housing Act of 1949 to provide city planners with greater flexibility in their urban redevelopment projects.

During the New Deal, therefore, housing reform under the guise of economic revival received official approval to the extent that the federal government had assumed the responsibilities of aiding private housing through the sponsorship of several programs designed to stimulate construction and of helping communities clear slums and replace them with low-cost, government-subsidized housing. Although the depression ended with the onset of the Second World War, these programs remained in effect and constituted the heart of the federal housing program for the next twenty-five years. But, like many New Deal programs, the federal housing activities were more significant for the new ideas that were adopted than for their actual achievements.[23]

Chapter II

Decent Housing for All

B Y THE TIME of America's entrance into the Second
World War, housing reform had made significant advances, mostly as a response to the depression. Encouraged by the gains of the thirties and bolstered by the political power of urban liberalism, housing reformers made a concerted effort during the war years to devise plans for a gigantic postwar attack on slums. The reformers aroused public enthusiasm through an extensive publicity campaign. They used the theme, "Plan now for postwar housing," and ambitiously set as their goal decent housing for all American families. "If we prepare adequately and if we act wisely and decisively, when the war is over, I believe we can inaugurate a housing reform program that will be worthy of the new era which will start when peace comes again," John B. Blandford, Jr., National Housing Agency administrator, exhorted his fellow reformers in 1943.[1] A subtheme of the program was the achievement of "unity" in postwar housing, that is, the reformers sought to establish a peaceful and profitable under-

standing with the private housing industry as to goals and methods. In recognizing the reform possibilities of public housing and slum clearance, they believed that a new age in urban life could be brought about.[2]

The significance of housing was made clear when the Roosevelt Administration, in taking its initial steps to prepare for war, secured passage of the Lanham Act in October of 1940, providing for the construction of 700,000 units of federal housing for defense workers. The real estate forces rallied in opposition to public housing and succeeded in having the act specify that all of the units had to be either sold or demolished immediately after the war; they could not be converted into low-income public housing. Although this program could not result in low-income public housing, it demonstrated to reformers the vast potentialities of a program of similar size, aimed at the elimination of slum housing. In other wartime moves, Congress inaugurated rent controls in 1942 and, to expedite the war housing endeavor, reorganized the various government housing agencies into the National Housing Agency.[3]

Prior to the war, housing reformers were relatively few in number. Much reform had been accomplished during the 1930's, but it had been achieved primarily under the guise of helping the housing industry recover from the depression.[4] During the war, however, greater interest in housing reform developed among the general public. Much of the enthusiasm was simply a result of individuals' plans and hopes for a home of their own. Next to his concern for a postwar job, reported Harry Bates, chairman of the American Federation of Labor's Housing Committee, the American GI wanted to know, "Will I have a home after the war?"[5] Naturally, this widespread public interest aided housing reform, and many new groups joined the ranks of the housing reformers: organized labor, veterans' organizations, ethnic and religious groups, local government officials, and federal housing officials. Support came also from such diverse groups as the League of

Women Voters, the Parents-Teachers Association, and the American Association of University Women. This new concern for housing reform found expression in many ways. "Housing weeks" were held; citizen groups conducted local discussion meetings; political leaders spoke; radio forums were broadcast; and theaters showed public information films. Public interest was maintained by an endless stream of articles in the daily newspapers, popular magazines, and professional housing journals.[6]

Initially, good leadership sparked the movement for postwar housing reform. Two prominent New York political leaders, Senator Robert F. Wagner and Mayor Fiorello LaGuardia, actively participated. Professional housing officials, such as Nathan Straus, former United States Housing administrator, and John B. Blandford, Jr., of the National Housing Agency, devoted much time and effort to the movement. Private citizens also became involved, as evidenced by the work of Dorothy Rosenman, wife of President Roosevelt's speech writer. Organized labor emphasized housing reform to its membership, and such labor leaders as Harry Bates of the A.F.L. and R. J. Thomas of the C.I.O. diligently campaigned for postwar housing.[7]

The reformers proposed no radically new programs. While emphasizing the need for public housing, they also suggested that urban redevelopment operate separately from public housing. Under the Wagner Housing Act of 1937, each unit of slum housing demolished had to be replaced by one unit of public housing. The reformers, however, realized that urban redevelopment could often serve a better purpose than merely providing public housing. Federal urban redevelopment programs, as now envisaged by the reformers, would provide funds for cities to purchase and clear slum areas. The local redevelopment authority would then have the option of building public housing, municipal buildings, or park areas or of reselling the land to private investors who could use the land as they desired, so long as their projects were acceptable to the city planning office and the local authority.[8]

In spite of the interest in urban redevelopment, public housing remained as the heart of the reform program. Early in the century, reformers had been reluctant to support this advanced type of housing reform because of its socialistic overtones, but by the end of the 1920's they realized that their tenement inspection laws and various other schemes had accomplished very little.[9] The shock of the depression ended all doubts and converted the reformers into public housing enthusiasts. During the 1930's social workers manned the vanguard of the public housing movement,[10] and their activities proved crucial in securing the passage of the Wagner Housing Act, the operations of which were interrupted by the war before they could begin to function effectively. The reformers based their public housing appeal upon the argument that private housing had "failed" to provide adequate housing for low-income families, who lived mainly in urban areas and comprised one fifth of the population of the United States. Because of the inequities inherent in the American economic system these families were unable to pay minimum rents for standard housing. Since the margin of profit was too small and the higher priced housing was more attractive to builders, the housing industry virtually ignored low-income housing. The owners of the tenements, the reformers continually emphasized, had a fine investment because of the low overhead costs, the low property taxes, and the steady income that these properties provided.[11]

In discussing the need for public housing, the reformers stressed the point that public housing would not hurt private housing. Only families unable to pay rents for decent housing would live in the government projects. Because private housing, as Wagner bluntly said, "has been and is unable to provide decent housing for families of low income at prices they can afford to pay,"[12] the federal government must accept the responsibility of providing this housing through the sponsorship of public housing projects. By furnishing such housing, the reformers argued, the nation would receive the untold benefits of an improved citizenry. The plight of the slum dweller no longer could be construed as a blessing in disguise, as Andrew Carnegie and Horatio Alger had once believed. The reformers documented with extensive data the relationship between poor housing and high crime and disease rates. Decent housing, they contended, would raise health standards, provide an atmosphere conducive to harmonious family life, and slash the high rates of social disorder associated with low-income areas. Such conditions would, in turn, elevate the standard of citizenship in these areas and encourage the residents to contribute more to their communities.[13]

The reformers also held that such a program would supplement the efforts of private housing and enable the nation to reach the goal of good housing for all. Public housing did not threaten the private housing industry; if the industry would provide adequate housing for families with low income, the reformers affirmed, they would happily abandon public housing. Expressing the view of the reformers before the Senate Subcommittee on Housing and Urban Redevelopment, Fiorello LaGuardia declared:

> We agree that ideally there should be no families with incomes too low to permit them to pay for adequate housing and purchase the other goods and services for a decent life. Until such time as our economic system provides such necessary income it is a clear function and duty of the government to see that no family has to live and rear its children in surroundings which are a disgrace to what we refer to with pride as the American standard of living.[14]

Even Philip N. Klutznick, Federal Public Housing commissioner, cherished the hope that public housing would never have to move up the income scale, but rather, that it would be forced progressively lower by good private housing.[15] A lower-ranking member of the public housing bureaucracy echoed this idea: "I hope that the time may come, in the not too distant future, when private enterprise may be able to do it all." He confessed that he never would have supported public housing "had not my own experiences over the years proved that there just seemed no other way to do it."[16]

Although the reform movement enjoyed good leadership, gained wide public support, and possessed considerable political influence, it lacked effective organization. Because no national reform league existed for the purpose of promoting postwar housing reform, the movement grew spontaneously. The National Housing Association had died early in the depression, and no similar organization took its place.[17] During the war a citizens group established the National Committee on Housing to publicize the need for postwar housing, but since its membership included both reformers and private housing officials, this organization served only as a convenient sounding board for different viewpoints, not as a useful vehicle for the accomplishments of specific reforms.[18] The only reform pressure group was the small National Public Housing Conference. Because its primary purpose was to promote public housing, the NPHC was not deeply concerned with other related programs. The conference suffered from shaky finances, small membership, limited purpose, and inability to develop grass-roots support.[19]

The private housing industry—realtors, builders, and lenders —responded quickly to the reformers' activities. Throughout the war the spokesmen for the industry were as energetic in discussing postwar housing as the reformers. Although eighteen trade associations comprised the housing industry, only three actively participated in the public discussions of the subject: the National Association of Real Estate Boards, the National Association of Home Builders, and the United States Savings and Loan League, each of which represented the major divisions of the mythical "housing industry."[20] The term "industry" is used only for want of a better, for the housing construction business was very disorganized. It had been almost unique in resisting centralization. Local contractors, often without sufficient capital, constructed only a few houses at a time and were reluctant to learn new construction methods or obtain better building materials to speed their work. Local building codes—usually outdated—often forced builders to use antiquated materials and methods. Similarly, the realtors were mostly small, local operators, who worked closely with the builders and lenders.[21] Believing that small firms rather than gigantic corporations embodied the true spirit of American free enterprise,[22] they prided themselves on their resistance to consolidation. It was not until the postwar years that the large-scale builders and the prefabrication companies developed.

The housing industry, as had most businesses, had suffered great financial losses during the depression. The production of houses dwindled to the century's low of only 93,000 units in 1933, and throughout the 1930's construction remained well below the peak years of the previous decade.[23] Many lending agencies were forced to liquidate or to close their doors temporarily. Since housing construction is vital to the economy of a nation, the industry received much attention from the government during the depression and, as previously remarked, benefited from several assistance programs designed to encourage house construction.[24]

Although these programs proved beneficial to the industry, they had a detrimental effect as well. Prior to the 1930's Americans usually turned to the business community for leadership, but the stock market crash of 1929 demonstrated the fallibility of the businessman. Throughout the depression the federal government assumed more and more of the responsibilities previously held by business and filled the leadership void.[25] Now, the government felt compelled to provide programs that would help the housing industry to revive and to assume its vital role in the nation's economy.[26]

The housing industry, however, because it remained pri-

marily localized and because it supposedly practiced the
virtues of self-reliance, free competition, and individual initiative, looked upon itself as both the embodiment of the true
spirit of the free enterprise system and its defender. This self-
created image clashed with reality. The government's various
programs, such as FHA and FSLIC, had been initiated because the industry had succumbed to the depression, and they
were maintained to prevent another disaster.[27] The inference
from these programs was that the housing industry needed a
permanent governmental crutch to prevent another fall. When
housing reformers spoke of the "failure" of private housing, the
reaction of the industry was resentment toward the government programs, which it labeled "bureaucratic interference."[28]
These programs, however, had aided business and promised
to produce stability and to provide a larger volume of construction in the postwar period. On the other hand, although
they were financially profitable, they were also a daily re-
minder to the industry of its lowered status. While the leaders
of the industry wanted these programs because they created
a higher volume of sales, they simultaneously detested the
idea that they were beneficial and, perhaps, essential.[29]

The industry resolved this dilemma by calling certain
government programs, such as FHA, "aids to private enterprise" because they fostered home ownership and contributed
to the stability of the housing business.[30] Blandly ignoring
the fact that FHA enabled realtors, lenders, and builders to
make substantial profits without risk, Herbert U. Nelson,
executive vice-president of the National Association of Real
Estate Boards, said: "In our country, we prefer that governmental activity shall take the form of assisting and aiding
private business rather than undertaking great public projects
of a governmental character."[31] By such a criterion, of all of the
government housing programs, only public housing did not
constitute "aid to private enterprise" because it did not encourage Americans to buy their own homes.

In actuality, public housing was not a threat to the industry, but it did symbolize the decline in the housing industry's prestige. Public housing, therefore, became a whipping boy for the frustrations of the industry as it confronted the wide chasm between its claims as a bulwark of competitive free enterprise and reality.[32] The industry's leaders devoted much effort and money to attempts to discredit public housing. They sought to show that public housing was not needed, that it would have a detrimental effect on the tenants' characters, and that it would lead to the demise of the private housing industry and, eventually, destroy the entire free enterprise system.

Because their opposition to public housing stemmed, to a large extent, from their emotions, the industry spokesmen often became hyperemotional in their attacks upon the institution. Public housing, they charged, was "European socialism in its most insidious form" and "the cutting edge of the Communist front."[33] As Congress prepared to pass the Housing Act of 1949, this irrationality led to such outbursts as: "All the fellow travelers are for the bill as the most subtle means of breaking down American self-reliance and American self-rule," and "We speak of Communism as the enemy, and it is. Gradually it seems to be winning some of our leaders from within."[34]

The industry naturally disliked the reformist argument that it could not provide decent housing for all Americans. Its spokesmen responded to reformers' charges of failure by contending that private housing could meet the nation's needs without the expense of public housing. The complex problem had a simple solution: the free operation of the private economy without government interference. By encouraging individual initiative with "aids for private enterprise," the greatest progress would result.[35] "This is the principle," said Arthur G. Erdman, president of the National Savings and Loan League, "on which our Country has grown great—the principle which has made our people as a whole the best housed, the best fed, the best served, the best paid, and the most enterprising and energetic in the world."[36] How would the low-income family be adequately housed? The answer was that, obviously, whenever a new house was built, a used one would become vacant; this would result in a "trickle-down" process, which would solve much of the problem. For those families whose income was so low that they could not pay the expected rent, local charity would grant them funds with which they could rent adequate housing of their own choosing.[37]

Because the reformers argued that public housing would improve the character of the tenants, the industry attempted to convince the public that the opposite would result. The private housing group, philosophically committed to a free economy in which the individual controls his own destiny, contended that federal subsidy would destroy individual initiative, encourage idleness by supporting those who are not self-reliant, create a class of citizens who would come to expect good housing as a reward for being poor, and thus undermine the free enterprise system.[38] Oscar Kreutz of the National Savings and Loan League emphasized this point before a Senate subcommittee:

> When we speak of the Government doing this and that we should keep in mind that, in our Democracy, the Government owns no capital that it can use for construction of housing facilities. What it donates to the Jones family—in whatever form and in whatever degree— must be taken from the pockets of the Smith family. Should the Smith families of the Country become discouraged and cease to be thrifty, not only would the Jones family not be provided with Governmental housing but the Smiths would be competing with the Joneses for governmental assistance. As a consequence, we should presently find ourselves in a position where we would all be consumers while but few would have sufficient incentive to continue as producers.[39]

Attacking public housing from another angle, the housing industry pictured it as a threat not only to the industry but also to the entire free economic system. "It is significant that in every country where economic planning and dictatorship have arisen in the last two decades, public housing on a large scale has been one of their first concerns," warned *Headlines,* the newsletter of the National Association of Real Estate Boards.[40] A representative of the National Association of Home Builders declared that his organization opposed public housing because it would "eventually destroy the entire building industry—dealers, financing institutions and builders." Public housing, he continued, was "the first step in the socialization of our country—the destruction of our democratic free-enterprise system. Unfortunately, like so many evils, a first step and a small dose is appealing and popular. Only by fully recognizing the social, political, and economic disaster which will come with its growth can one properly gauge the eventual result."[41] The industry's representatives claimed also that public housing was unfair because it placed the government in direct competition with individual citizens. Joseph E. Merrion of the National Association of Home Builders stated:

> We do not concede the need or the right of the Federal Government, either directly or by subsidy to local housing authorities, to enter the housing field by building, owning or operating permanent housing projects. We feel that in doing so, the Government is invading the field of private enterprise, setting itself up in the business of competition with citizens and taxpayers.[42]

Public housing was "paternalistic federal encroachment in the field of housing and local affairs," *Headlines* concluded.[43]

Private housing also feared the consequences of the proposed slum clearance program. Spokesmen for the industry readily agreed with the reformers that some method had to be devised to solve the slum problem, since slums covered over 25 per cent of all urban area in the United States.[44] The industry feared, however, the application of the "equivalent elimination" provision of the Wagner Housing Act.[45] Although local redevelopment authorities, under the proposed new legislation, would no longer be tied to public housing and could use federal funds to buy and clear the slum areas and then resell them to private developers, the private housing group disliked the important role the federal government would play in such transactions. They were apprehensive that in actual practice only public housing would replace cleared slums. At the same time, the housing industry admitted that private capital was totally unable to conduct an urban re-development program on the scale that the situation de-manded and therefore gave its approval, although carefully guarded, to the new slum clearance plan.[46]

The private housing group, in presenting its position, nec-essarily drew a blurred line between the highly desirable "aids for private enterprise" and the repugnant "paternalism" of public housing. While private housing hailed the con-tinuation and expansion of FHA and the adoption of "yield insurance," which would ensure builders of large rental apart-ments at least 3 per cent annual profit, it resolutely opposed public housing for the low-income family on the grounds that it would stifle initiative and ruin character. What the industry desired, apparently, was governmental props that would re-move all risk from the housing business, guarantee a steady volume of sales, and stimulate housing construction in the high-income areas where larger profits were possible. Just how committed private housing actually was to competition and individual risk is an intriguing question. Although the industry used such terms as "free enterprise" and "individual-ism" in their arguments against public housing, the restora-tion of unrestricted competition without governmental par-ticipation was the last thing it wanted. It found in public housing a convenient foe that had the necessary elements of a possible threat and that neatly symbolized the frustrations resulting from the intrusion of the government into the hous-ing field. Thus, because public housing accomplished a task that private housing was not capable of performing, because it did have certain aspects that might lead in the future to the government's expansion into the housing field, and because it symbolized an important loss of prestige, the housing industry developed an extensive publicity campaign to eradicate the program.

The industry's real estate lobby became one of the most effective pressure groups in Washington. The various trade associations organized into the Realtor's Washington Committee, through which they correlated their political activities. Herbert U. Nelson, a long-time Washington lobbyist, skillfully directed the committee's activities. Because the trade associations had active membership in almost every community, Nelson was able to use the grass-roots method of pressuring Congress. On any given day Nelson could flood Congress with letters, telegrams, and telephone calls from prominent citizens in all parts of the nation. Because many of the members of the lobby were prominent citizens in their communities and spent large sums of money on local advertising, they often persuaded their communities' newspapers to publish editorials supporting the crusade against public housing. Such editorials, brought to the attention of the community's representative in Congress, supposedly carried much influence.[47]

The industry, therefore, actively participated in the general discussion of postwar housing. Its leaders, just as those of the reformers, wrote articles, spoke at public meetings, testified before congressional hearings, and conducted other similar activities to present the lobby's position. Although this participation added zest to the issue, it clearly indicated that the desired "unity in housing" would never be achieved.

The national interest in postwar housing naturally led to congressional action. As part of the Servicemen's Readjustment Act of 1944, Congress included a provision through which the Veterans Administration could guarantee as much as 55 per cent of home loans to veterans of the Second World War.[48] This section of the "GI Bill of Rights" greatly aided veterans in buying homes immediately after the war and thereby added considerably to the already high demand for houses. In part, this program led to the frantic construction of the often criticized "package suburbs" during the postwar period.[49]

Despite the importance of the GI bill, Congress devoted most of its attention to the problems of slum clearance and of low-income housing. Early in 1943 the Senate created the Special Subcommittee on Housing and Urban Redevelopment, which conducted extensive hearings to gather information from which a legislative program for postwar housing could be prepared.[50] Although public interest in housing figured prominently in the formation of this subcommittee, a power struggle within the government was the immediate motivation for its creation.

The Seventy-eighth Congress, elected in November of 1942, contained many opponents of the New Deal; in fact, several of the members had campaigned as staunch anti-New Dealers.[51] These congressmen coupled their anti-New Dealism with the belief that the Roosevelt Administration exercised powers that rightfully belonged to Congress. These factors led to a concerted congressional attack upon the National Resources Planning Board, an advisory body established in 1934-1935 by Roosevelt to plan long-range economic programs. When Roosevelt announced that he had received the NRPB *Report* for 1943, which contained detailed proposals for postwar planning, the House of Representatives promptly dissolved the board by refusing to appropriate its annual operating funds.[52] "This vicious body," as Republican Congressman Frederick C. Smith (Ohio) described the NRPB,[53] served as an ideal target for opponents of the Administration because it symbolized both the usurpation of congressional prerogatives by the Administration and "socialistic" New Deal planning. Many congressmen readily agreed with Republican Congressman Everett Dirksen (Ill.) that "the burden and responsibility for the continued planning rests entirely with the Congress and nowhere else."[54]

Roosevelt, fully aware of the unhappiness in Congress with the National Resources Planning Board, did not release the NRPB *Report* immediately. He preferred to wait and see what the opposition would do.[55] Just before the House dissolved the board, Roosevelt made a clever political move. At a press conference he remarked, "I don't care how planning is done. They can abolish the National Resources Planning Board if they set up some other organization to do the work. It is perfectly immaterial as to who does it, as long as it gets done." And, he carefully emphasized, "That is up to the Congress."[56] By issuing this statement, Roosevelt absolved his Administration from the arduous task of preparing the postwar program and placed the responsibility squarely upon Congress. He released the NRPB *Report* a few days after the House had killed the NRPB and reiterated his conviction that planning would help avert a postwar economic disaster. He promised Congress the full cooperation of his Administration.[57]

Just two days later, the Senate created the Special Committee on Postwar Policy and Planning.[58] The original resolution for the committee underscored the jealousy in Congress that was expressed in the move: "This resolution recognizes the responsibility of the Congress to the people of the United States for our postwar economic planning."[59] The Senate, in order to prevent New Deal liberals from dominating the committee, named as its chairman Walter George, one of the Southern senators whom Roosevelt had attempted to purge in 1938.[60]

The attack in Congress upon liberal planning, as evinced by the NRPB episode, clashed with the housing reform movement. Congress could not ignore housing because of the intense national concern, but it did not want to allow the program to be dominated by such a leading Keynesian economist as Alvin Hansen, the housing expert on the NRPB. The Senate therefore created the Special Subcommittee on Housing and Urban Redevelopment under George's committee and instructed it to examine all aspects of postwar housing. To prevent a "socialistic" program from being adopted, the Senate entrusted the committee chairmanship to Republican Robert A. Taft of Ohio, who had denounced the NRPB *Report* as "a combination of hooey and false promises."[61]

Because the war was far from over, the senators postponed indefinitely the subcommittee's activities. Before Taft finally began hearings in the middle of 1944, Roosevelt demonstrated his awareness of the public interest in housing by sending an enthusiastic letter to the 1944 meeting of the National Committee on Housing, in which he urged planning for the purpose of reaching the goal of decent housing for all income groups.[62] In his 1944 State of the Union message—his controversial Economic Bill of Rights—Roosevelt added his voice to the growing demand in the nation for good housing.[63] This speech, drawing heavily upon the final report of the National Resources Planning Board, gave Presidential endorsement to the movement for public housing—something that had been absent in the 1930's.

The ensuing hearings of the Taft subcommittee produced no startling new ideas, but they did bring into perspective the various programs and ideas being discussed throughout the nation. As the hearings progressed, early in 1945 under Taft's methodical chairmanship, there emerged considerable understanding between the private housing industry and the reformers. Both groups recognized the existence of a housing shortage that would increase sharply at the end of the war and that could be met only by an unprecedented program of construction. Although several different estimates were made, most people accepted the National Housing Agency's prediction that 12,600,000 units would be needed in the first decade following the war.[64] The reformers and the industry's leaders also concurred upon the desirability of reaching the reformers' goal of good housing for every family and of giving private housing every opportunity to accomplish this end.[65] They further agreed that the federal government should play an important role by providing several programs to assist private housing in meeting this goal. Such government programs should include the continuation of FHA mortgage loan insurance and of the Federal Home Loan Bank, a new government program of "yield insurance," which would ensure a fair annual profit for builders of apartments for middle-income families, and a research program to develop new building materials and construction methods.[66] Predictably, the only major source of disagreement was public housing.

After gathering over two thousand pages of testimony from more than fifty witnesses, the hearings ended on February 7, 1945. Although no new startling ideas or programs had been presented, the hearings were of great significance in the history of housing reform. The thoroughness of the subcommittee and the length of the investigation demonstrated the importance Americans now placed on housing reform. Housing was no longer a local matter, as the enormous costs involved demanded that the federal government use its vast resources to help conquer the slum problem. The question now asked by the subcommittee was not whether the government should act, but how. The hearings were important also because they assembled in one place a mass of data that clearly pointed to the complex problems involved in the field of housing.

The subcommittee postponed delivering its report for almost six months. The leaders of the subcommittee—Taft, Wagner, and Allen J. Ellender (Dem., La.)—waited until legislation could be drafted by Wagner's legislative aides to allow the report and the bill to be made public simultaneously. This was done on August 1, 1945; Taft presented the subcommittee's report, and Wagner and Ellender introduced the comprehensive housing bill, which incorporated the subcommittee's major recommendations.[67] The two sponsors realized that Congress would not pass the bill in the form presented; they hoped that, by giving congressmen an opportunity to study the report together with the bill during the congressional recess scheduled to begin the next day, Congress would be forced to focus its attention upon postwar housing when it reconvened. The subcommittee's report, based upon the assumption that "from the social point of view, a supply of good housing, sufficient to meet the needs of all families, is essential to a sound and stable democracy," followed the reform position closely. Because poor housing is "a deterrent to the development of a sound citizenry," the subcommittee recommended a "comprehensive" bill designed to meet the needs of all citizens. The report, consequently, urged that a large public housing program be inaugurated, that federal funds be used to redevelop slum areas, and that a national housing policy be adopted to state clearly the government's obligation to provide each citizen with an opportunity to enjoy decent housing. Within this "comprehensive" framework, the report also called for a housing research program, loans to builders of middle-income homes, liberalization of FHA lending policies, a new program of "yield insurance," and the reorganization of the National Housing Agency into a permanent government agency.[68]

In accordance with its original assumption the subcommittee emphasized the responsibilities of private housing, but pointed out that the industry's failure to provide "decent" housing for low-income families left the government no alternative but to sponsor public housing. "The justification for public housing must rest on the proposition that the Federal Government has an interest in seeing that minimum standards of housing, food, and health services are available for all members of the community," the subcommittee concluded.[69]

The subcommittee's report and the Wagner-Ellender bill climaxed a widespread movement during the war to prepare plans for a vast postwar housing program. The reformers' attempts to create a national consensus for housing reform had succeeded. A program had been devised, and a detailed bill embodying the goals of the reformers had been introduced in

Congress. Housing reformers were soon to applaud the somewhat surprising development of vigorous Presidential leadership for their program. As Americans pondered the implications of Hiroshima and Nagasaki and cheered the news of V-J Day, Samuel I. Rosenman, Franklin D. Roosevelt's former aide and speech writer for twenty years, was busily drafting one of the most significant Presidential documents of the postwar period, which, among other things, placed the new President at the head of the housing reform movement.

Chapter III

Truman Assumes Leadership

HARRY S TRUMAN was the first President to support housing reform actively and enthusiastically. Theodore Roosevelt had endorsed tenement inspection when he was governor of New York, but he had turned to other matters during his Presidency. Herbert Hoover summoned a national conference on housing in 1931, but his motive was to infuse new life into the severely depressed construction industry, not to reform it. During his first two terms of office, Franklin D. Roosevelt paid little attention to housing; although he did not oppose housing reform, he was not an outspoken advocate of the movement. Quite understandably, he also viewed housing reform primarily as an economic stimulant.[1] After the full implications of the 1940 election were realized—that his political future was dependent upon the urban vote—Roosevelt became more interested in housing reform. Even though the war sharply limited his attention to domestic affairs, he did include the goal of good housing for all income groups in his Economic Bill of Rights in 1944.

This single endorsement filled housing reformers with enthusiasm and created great expectations for the postwar era.

On April 12, 1945, however, Roosevelt died, and the responsibilities of leadership descended upon Harry S Truman. For almost eight years Truman wrestled with the many problems left unsolved by Roosevelt and with the innumerable ones that arose during his terms of office. Truman inherited not only the strength of Roosevelt's urban coalition but also the burden of the anti-New Deal coalition. He realized that his party's future rested with the urban areas and therefore carefully shaped his Fair Deal to maintain the urban-Democratic alliance and to strengthen his political position. This he did, to a large extent, through the inclusion of ample provisions for housing reform in his program. The election of 1948 proved how well he assessed national opinion.

Although Truman recognized the political necessity of supporting housing reform, his support did not result solely from this motivation; it stemmed also from his genuine concern for "the people."[2] Sincerely believing that housing reform constituted a need that could no longer be neglected, he fused his practical politics with his own predispositions and personally provided the driving force within his Administration for this relatively new area of federal reform.

The President's own experiences in his varied career had inculcated into his political philosophy a sympathetic understanding of the everyday problems of the American laborer, small businessman, and farmer and had led him into the ranks of urban liberalism. His genuine concern for "the people" formed a basis for his Fair Deal. His association with the veterans of the First World War had given him insight into the problems of the dislocations of postwar adjustment[3] and undoubtedly had influenced his determination to aid the veterans of the Second World War. His practical brand of liberalism, developed out of his own business failures and his encounters with the working class, helped establish a common bond of understanding with the American populace and impelled him to help them.[4] As a judge in Jackson County, Missouri, he had become involved with the problems of welfare during the depression years and had supported the plan to construct a new courthouse in order to provide needed work for many unemployed citizens.[5] His experiences as a judge also exposed him to certain housing problems, especially those related to zoning laws, while the building of the courthouse introduced him to the many technical problems of construction work.[6] He was a staunch supporter of the New Deal and had voted for most New Deal programs while he was in the Senate. He later maintained that the New Deal was similar to the program he had followed on the local level as a judge.[7] In 1937 Senator Truman voted for the Wagner Housing Act, and one of the problems with which his famous war-production committee had wrestled was that of defense housing. This investigational experience furnished Truman with detailed knowledge of the complexities involved in housing construction and prompted him to write, in the autumn of 1944 as he campaigned for the Vice-Presidency, that housing and urban redevelopment would be one of the major problems facing postwar America. He declared, "The heart of a community is its housing," and only a massive postwar federal housing program would "secure the greater welfare of the individual citizen."[8] As President, he enthusiastically pushed the most important reform of urban liberalism at this time: a broad program of urban redevelopment and public housing.

Political considerations alone, then, did not motivate Truman to include housing in his Message on Reconversion, which he sent to Congress on September 6, 1945. This message, which contained the core of what Truman later called his Fair Deal, included twenty-one proposals for the "reconversion" period.[9] Written by Samuel I. Rosenman at Truman's request, it marked the transition from the New Deal to the Fair Deal. Truman selected Rosenman because "he was familiar with the facts and philosophy of the New

Deal."[10] Because of its content, tone, and authorship, this message symbolizes the close relationship between the two Democratic reform programs.

In the eleventh point of this message Truman diagrammed for Congress his housing program. He drew upon the precedents of the New Deal experiments, the 1943 National Resources Planning Board *Report*, Roosevelt's Economic Bill of Rights, and, especially, the *Report* of the Senate Subcommittee on Housing and Urban Redevelopment. He told the Congress that his goal, a decent house for every American family, could be achieved only by the enactment of a comprehensive housing bill that included public housing, slum clearance, liberal aids to private housing, and the adoption of a national housing policy affirming the government's responsibility in postwar housing. "A decent standard of housing for all is one of the irreducible obligations of modern civilization," Truman declared. "The people of the United States, so far ahead in wealth and production capacity, deserve to be the best housed in the world. We must begin to meet that challenge at once."[11] Truman's housing program placed him in the front ranks of the housing reform movement and, together with his other domestic reforms, demonstrated his desire to become the national leader of urban liberalism.

The Message on Reconversion clearly established the congressional battle lines. Until Truman dispatched this message to Congress, many members of the antiwelfare coalition had believed that the new border-state President would follow their leadership and begin a movement away from the New Deal, federal welfare programs, and reform activity.[12] But the message quickly burst this bubble of conservative hope. As Truman later told Jonathan Daniels, he intended that this message would "let the Hearsts and McCormicks know that they were not going to take me into camp."[13] Joe Martin, one of the coalition leaders, typified the conservative reaction:

A long decade, more or less, had passed since our struggles against the alphabet agencies, government handouts, and socialist experiments. . . . At last the time seemed propitious in spite of disruption on all sides for a gradual advance toward sound, conservative, non-meddling government. But here we were being urged back on the same dreary old circuit of paternalism, controls, spending, high taxes, and vague objectives.

The Truman program, Martin told newsmen at this time, was "just a plain case of out-New Dealing the New Deal."[14]

On November 14, 1945, three senators introduced a bill that incorporated Truman's housing program.[15] This single bill contained: a national housing policy, a system of "yield insurance" for large-scale investors in middle-income rentals, various changes in the lending powers of home loan banks to bring them into line with the GI bill, provisions for housing research, relaxed Federal Housing Administration insurance terms, loans to farmers for home improvements, extensive federal aid to urban redevelopment, and construction of a half-million units of public housing, to be built over a four-year period. The sponsors—Robert F. Wagner, Robert A. Taft, and Allen J. Ellender—had devoted much attention to the housing problem, and their varied political philosophies, sectional differences, and partisanship had enabled most of the aspects of the issue to be incorporated into the bill.

Taft, a leading critic of the New Deal and an aspirant to the Presidency, led the conservative Republicans in Congress. At the heart of his conservatism lay a commitment to a free economy and local responsibility. Although many conservatives shunned public housing, he had long expressed an interest in it and had incorporated it into his political philosophy.[16] Price controls, he held, were unjustified interference in the free economy, but public housing would not restrict the free system and, more important, would be locally initiated and controlled; the federal government would only provide the funds. As early as February, 1942, Taft had told the Senate that he believed a very extensive federal housing program would soon have to be inaugurated because the high costs of urban redevelopment would prohibit local or state governments from carrying out the task.[17] Private housing, as Taft had seen from his own experience in slum-ridden Cincinnati, would also lack the financial resources to undertake the job. Therefore, federal aid must be made available to provide decent housing for the low-income families.[18] Taft's conservative approach to housing reform, however, demanded assurances that public housing would never invade the territory of private housing. Public housing must serve only those families that could not afford to provide their own housing. Taft carefully studied cost tables to calculate the minimum cost of acceptable housing standards; he was determined that public housing would not become, in any aspect, luxury housing.[19] Much of the Ohioan's attitude was based upon the doctrine of the earlier reform movement—good housing is a prerequisite to good citizenship. He saw the happy, healthy family as a microcosm of democracy; because the family is the cornerstone upon which the United States has been built, good housing is vital.

Taft's role as a sponsor of the Truman housing program was threefold. He gave the bill bipartisan sponsorship and led the Republican group that supported the bill. In the Senate about twenty Republicans, who came largely from urban states, consistently followed Taft's leadership. Taft also gave the bill the endorsement of respectable conservatism and was often cited by the bill's supporters as an example of an enlightened conservative who saw public housing in its correct perspective. Taft served, too, as a brake upon more avid enthusiasts for public housing who would have liked a far more expansive program. Many conservatives, however, did not follow Taft's leadership and, as they watched his housing activities, could only mutter, "Taft is becoming a damn Socialist."[20]

Allen J. Ellender, a product of the Huey Long machine,

had replaced the "Kingfish" in the Senate in 1936. Ellender mixed New Deal liberalism with intense segregation. He sponsored the second Agricultural Adjustment Act, supported Roosevelt's attack upon the Supreme Court of the United States, and favored the Fair Labor Standards Act—but only after he had received special considerations for employers in the South. Ellender had, by conducting a six-day filibuster, personally defeated a bill that sought in 1937 to outlaw lynching and had opposed all legislation to remove the poll tax requirement and to establish a permanent Fair Employment Practices Commission.[21] Zealously supporting a comprehensive approach to housing, he had voted for the Wagner Housing Act and, according to Wagner, had been a "staunch and effective friend of public housing in the Senate since the day he arrived in Washington."[22] Ellender believed housing to be the single most important domestic question in the postwar period. Because his own political strength lay with the lower classes of Louisiana, he was familiar with the slum conditions in the South and viewed public housing as a means of alleviating this rapidly increasing problem, especially for Negro families.[23] Ellender was typical of a large number of Southern senators who became supporters of the Administration's housing program. Most southern cities had chronic slum problems and experienced serious housing shortages for low-income families. These senators looked upon federal aid to housing and slum clearance as the most effective and inexpensive way to solve these problems. Significantly, the issue of segregation in housing did not become important enough during Truman's Administration to cause these southerners any embarrassment.

In contrast to the position of the Southern senators, the Southern representatives stood in opposition to housing legislation and were instrumental in preventing, for three years, passage of the bill. This group, composed of about fifty congressmen, opposed the bill for three basic reasons. Since most of these legislators represented predominantly rural districts and had no worries concerning the urban vote, they were, on the whole, unaware of and unconcerned about urban problems. They refused to believe that the problems of slums and poor housing could not be solved locally. Quite understandably, many of them did not support this huge program of federal spending because it would pour millions of dollars into areas that they did not represent. Their opposition was rooted also in a genuine fear of big government; they felt that they must guard against the establishment of an extensive federal bureaucracy, which the bill would necessarily expand.[24] The Democratic party in the South, therefore, split on the housing issue. While almost all of the senators from the South and most of the representatives from the urban districts of the region favored Truman's program, the congressmen from rural areas adamantly opposed it.

While Taft and Ellender played important roles in formulating and supporting Truman's housing program, Senator Robert F. Wagner spearheaded the urban liberals' campaign for its adoption. He provided forceful leadership and, until he retired from the Senate in 1949, devoted much of his energy to the bill. Wagner probably knew more about housing than any other legislator; certainly, no one was more concerned with the problem than he. During the New Deal he sponsored the National Industrial Recovery Act, the Federal Emergency Relief Act, the National Labor Relations Act, and the Social Security Act,[25] and in 1937 he secured passage of the United States Housing Act. Wagner was quite proud of his housing act, for he saw it as a partial embodiment of his basic creed that every American should enjoy certain fundamental rights, among them decent housing. "Since I have been in Washington," he said, "I have sought to establish the basic guarantees for the average American family: Security against want in unemployment and in old age . . . security of home ownership and thorough decent housing conditions."[26] Yet, despite his enthusiasm for public housing, Wagner placed primary emphasis upon private housing: "We want private enterprise

to do the largest possible share of the total housing job."
Public housing, he continually stressed, should merely supplement the efforts of private housing. The only way America
could attain its housing goal, he continued, was by working
closely with the private housing industry. Until private housing could serve the low-income families, however, public
housing would have to play a vital part in the nation's housing
market. Public housing was, to this dedicated servant of the
urban lower classes, "the test of our determination to make
democracy work."[27]

Wagner's interest went beyond the desire for decent housing. He believed that the postwar period held a serious threat
of widespread unemployment, and he wanted a large government program to be ready to stimulate the economy and sus-
tain full employment. While he worked for the housing
bill, he also cosponsored the Employment Act of 1946. He
had argued for the 1937 Housing Act as primarily an economic program and argued for the Wagner-Ellender-Taft bill
in similar terms.[28]

These three senators, therefore, joined together to draft
and sponsor the Administration's housing bill. On November
14, 1945, they took advantage of the mushrooming nationwide housing shortage to dramatize the importance of their
bill. "The housing shortage now facing the country is critical
to the point of emergency," Wagner informed the Senate.
"However, it should not be dealt with by emergency legislation. . . . It is high time that we stop improvision, get a true
perspective of the whole problem, and work out a sound,
long-term solution."[29] Ellender spoke at length upon the
bill's purpose and emphasized the sponsors' attempts to provide a program that would not alter the traditional role of
private housing. The bill, he said, would actually enable
private housing to do a better job. It was "a fair bill—fair to
every interest group, including private enterprise, public officials, and others who have a legitimate and progressive
interest in providing decent housing for the American peo-

ple."[30] Taft discussed the basic assumption of the bill that the government had to assume a responsibility in housing. He urged the Senate to support the bill because, as he said, "We have an interest in seeing that there is provided for every family in the country at least a minimum shelter, of a decent character, which will enable the American family to develop."[31]

Although the sponsors called their legislation a "private enterprise bill," the housing industry refused to accept the section on public housing. By including provision for the construction of a half-million units of public housing in a bill that provided many programs desired by the housing industry, the sponsors deftly presented the industry with a dilemma. The bill gave the industry an "all or nothing" alternative: Accept the detested public housing or receive none of the other attractive programs.[32] *Headlines* had warned its realtor readers of such a possibility in June: "It is daily more apparent that the Wagner-Ellender-Taft bill, which ought to be introduced fairly soon, will sandwich a layer of new public housing between substantial slices of aid to private enterprise."[33] Within a few days after the introduction of the bill *Headlines* questioned the need for public housing, on the ground that it would take away vital building materials at a time when a severe housing shortage existed. The bill, the newsletter continued, would place the government irrevocably in the housing field, even though private housing was capable of serving all income groups if freed from interference and restrictions.[34] The NAREB convention, held in November, decided that all the government aid was not worth the price of approving public housing and unanimously condemned the legislation.[35]

Within three months after the defeat of Japan, therefore, Congress began consideration of a housing bill that sought to initiate an active government program by which the goal of a well-housed America would be reached within a decade. The bill, a product of lengthy hearings, had been blessed by bipartisan sponsorship and a warm Presidential endorsement. Now it was sent to the Senate Banking and Currency Committee for study; with it went the hopes of housing reformers and urban liberals. Meanwhile, the private housing industry mobilized its influential real estate lobby to launch a counterattack. With the preliminaries concluded, the main battle was about to begin.

Chapter IV

The Year of Frustration

A T THE END of the Second World War, as millions of servicemen returned home, an unprecedented housing shortage, considered by many to be a "national calamity,"[1] engulfed the nation. The problem was simply one of numbers: too many families, too few homes. The rural-to-urban migration to man the war industries further complicated matters; defense workers, reluctant to return to their home towns, remained in the cities. In Los Angeles, for example, fewer than 15 per cent of the 782,000 war workers left the city. Since the average veteran had a limited income and little, if any, savings, the bulk of the housing demand centered on low- and middle-cost urban housing. Unfortunately, this type of housing was the most difficult to provide; the small margin of profit that it offered did not attract private builders. About 75 per cent of the 5 million families seeking homes could afford no more than $50 a month in rent, and they could pay no more than $6,000 for a house. Thus, the veteran in his individual search for housing and the Truman

Administration in its nationwide program to provide it faced an abnormally large demand for inexpensive housing, of which there was a distressingly low supply.[2]

Throughout the nation many veterans and their families lived in attics, basements, chicken coops, and boxcars. Washington, D.C., for example, reported 25,000 homeless veterans; Chicago had four times that number, while relatively small Jefferson City, Missouri, needed 500 homes for returned servicemen. In Atlanta, 2,000 persons answered one advertisement of a vacancy, and a want ad in an Omaha newspaper read, "Big Ice Box, 7 by 17 feet. Could be fixed up to live in." Even if the veteran found an apartment, he often had to pay a "tip" of $100 or more before he could sign the lease. Often until he located a place to live, the veteran and his family moved in with relatives or friends. As he searched, he soon realized that his reward for helping to win the war did not include a decent place to live. There arose an anguished cry of betrayal from the homeless veterans. "It's the same old story," one disgruntled corporal snarled. "You fight a goddam war and you finally come home and everybody slaps you on the back and tells you what a wonderful job you did and all that crap, but when it comes to really doing something, then nobody's home. All you get is words." Out of this bitterness there soon arose from most segments of American society a demand for action. With the politically powerful veterans' organizations in the lead, the housing issue was forced onto the front pages of the newspapers and into the halls of Congress. The aroused public bombarded Congress and the White House with cries for immediate action. Thus, inadequate housing, affecting several million families directly, created a sense of urgency for housing reform—something most other Fair Deal programs lacked.[3]

The Truman Administration responded to this crisis with a twofold program. It created the office of Housing Expediter to conduct the Veterans' Emergency Housing Program, which attempted to facilitate rapid construction of low-cost housing for veterans. President Truman, realizing that the VEHP was to be short-lived, endorsed and actively supported, as the second part of his housing program, the Wagner-Ellender-Taft bill. By the end of 1946, however, Congress had rejected the W-E-T bill, and the VEHP had disintegrated in the wake of the November congressional elections.

In October, 1945, the Truman Administration attempted to stimulate home construction by removing wartime restrictions on the use of building materials. The person responsible for this premature move was John W. Snyder, director of the Office of War Mobilization and Reconversion. Snyder had been one of Truman's closest friends ever since they had met by chance in France during the First World War. After the war they had spent many weeks together in summer encampments of the Army Reserve. While Truman dabbled in business and politics, Snyder pursued a career in banking, serving his apprentice years with small-town banks in Missouri and in his native Arkansas. In 1930 Snyder assumed a position with the federal Office of the Comptroller of the Currency, and for the next seven depression-ridden years he processed the failures of Missouri banks as they went into receivership. In 1937 he was appointed to the directorship of the St. Louis Loan Agency of the Reconstruction Finance Corporation and in 1940 moved to Washington, D.C., to serve as assistant to the director of RFC and to work in Jesse Jones's National Defense Plant Corporation. He returned to private banking in 1943 and assumed the vice-presidency of the First National Bank of St. Louis. It was from this position that Truman summoned him to Washington on the night of Franklin D. Roosevelt's death.[4]

Snyder's banking experience to a large extent determined his economic and political philosophy. By any standard of measurement he stood somewhere right of center. An outspoken opponent of government planning of the New Deal variety, he identified himself as a "profit-system man" and believed that "the very foundation of American Democracy is private initiative."[5] *The New York Times,* in a biographical sketch of Snyder, pointed out, "Those earnest and troubled citizens who for the last twelve years have decried the absence of an atmosphere in Washington hospitable to the needs and interest of business should be heartened to know their wish is in the process of realization."[6]

Snyder's hasty action in removing controls from building materials on October 15, 1945, effected a construction boom but produced very little housing. This boom resulted in "a rash of race tracks, mansions, summer resorts, bowling alleys, stores and cocktail bars," remarked Housing Expediter Wilson Wyatt. "Yes, it was a fine building boom, except nobody much was bothering to build any homes that veterans could afford."[7] Just forty days after Truman lifted the controls, Snyder, confronted by wrathful veterans, advised the President to restore them. On December 12 the Director of the Office of War Mobilization and Reconversion, although deeply devoted to a free and unrestricted economy, recommended not only a restoration of price controls but also strict allocation of building materials and imposition of a ceiling upon the cost of new homes. At the advice of his close friend and top economic adviser Truman placed a $10,000 ceiling on all new homes and ordered the Office of War Mobilization and Reconversion to channel no less than 50 per cent of all construction materials into housing. Finally, at Snyder's suggestion, Truman created the Office of Housing Expediter within OWMR to direct a crash program designed to relieve the situation as rapidly as possible.[8]

Truman persuaded Wilson Wyatt, a liberal Democrat who had served successfully as mayor of Louisville (1941-1945), to decline a lucrative position with a corporation law firm and to become Housing Expediter. Wyatt had attracted nationwide attention for his progressive administration during the war. His outstanding work in slum clearance and city planning prompted Dorothy Rosenman, chairman of the National Committee on Housing, to suggest to Truman that

Wyatt be appointed Housing Expediter. Assuring Wyatt of his complete support, Truman told him to "make no little plans" and instructed him to "search out all bottlenecks at whatever level of industry or of Government, . . . [to] break those bottlenecks, and make the machinery of housing production run as smoothly as possible, so that we may be able to make the peace production of homes equal to the task of housing our veterans and other civilians."[9] Within a short period Truman again expressed his confidence in Wyatt by appointing him successor to John B. Blandford, Jr., administrator of the National Housing Agency.[10]

Encouraged by Truman's exhortation to "use every agency and every resource of the Government" and armed with wartime emergency powers, Wyatt immersed himself in a round of conferences with leaders of government, business, labor, and veterans' groups. He told the nation, upon assuming his office, "The housing shortage is a tough nut to crack, [but] with patience and good will on the part of everyone concerned, much can be done to relieve it right now and to lick it in the not too distant future."[11]

After five weeks of intent study of the situation, Wyatt sent the resultant report to the President. On February 8, 1946, Truman announced, with much fanfare, that he wholeheartedly supported his expediter's program: "He has recommended a Veterans' Emergency Housing Program which is bold, vigorous and eminently practical. It has the complete and unqualified support of the Administration." Wyatt, envisaging a goal of 2,700,000 homes to be built within two years, developed his program around the use of strong federal controls. The major provisions of the program stipulated strict allocation of scarce materials, maintenance of rent controls within 3 per cent of the prewar level, $600 million in "premium payments" to encourage high-volume production of scarce building materials, and Reconstruction Finance Corporation loans to the infant industry of factory-made houses to enable it to produce 750,000 homes by the end of 1947.[12]

Wyatt based his program upon the premise that the war-produced housing shortage could be relieved only by the utilization of wartime emergency controls. If uncontrolled, the building industry would produce homes to be sold above the price most veterans could afford. "It will take a dynamic program to achieve this goal," Wyatt informed Truman. "Neither business-as-usual, labor-as-usual, building-as-usual, nor government-as-usual will suffice."[13] Despite the national wish that wartime restrictions be removed, Wyatt moved boldly to continue and expand such controls. Because of the acuteness of the shortage he was striving to relieve, the controls at first received general acceptance, but as the year progressed, first the business community, then public opinion, and finally the White House showed increasing dissatisfaction with them.

Because the Second War Powers Act, from which the VEHP derived its power, expired June 30, 1946, Congress needed to pass legislation enabling the program to go into permanent operation. When the bill, sponsored by Congressman Wright Patman (Dem., Tex.), moved through the legislative mill, its opponents launched an assault upon its key provisions. The "back-to-normalcy" conservatives in Congress, opposing the idea of continued controls, vigorously attacked both the proposed ceiling on new homes and the allocation of building materials as being contrary to the free economic system and not within the framework of a free society in peacetime.[14] These congressmen did not agree with Wyatt's insistence upon wartime controls; they argued that a return to an unrestricted economy would build homes faster than "bureaucratic red tape" and that housing would become bogged down in endless administrative detail if the program was enacted. The conservatives, led by Jesse Wolcott (Rep., Mich.), Frederick C. Smith (Rep., Ohio), and Carl Hinshaw (Rep., Calif.), found premium payments the most vulnerable targets; these "subsidies," as they called them, simply rewarded inefficiency and opened up new areas for governmental favoritism. Such use of federal funds, they insisted, would enable Wyatt to become a "dictator" and allow him to enrich any company he desired.

In the House of Representatives the conservatives successfully stripped both premium payments and ceiling prices from the bill despite the President's plea, made publicly to Speaker of the House Sam Rayburn, and despite Wyatt's charge that "selfish interest" wished "to perpetuate the housing shortage to gain speculative profits from inflationary real estate profits." After the setback in the House Truman, at a press conference, reiterated his desire to get the original bill through Congress: "Whatever it takes we will proceed to do, to get that program put through. That is one we are really behind, with everything we have."[15]

The Senate, far more friendly to the VEHP, restored the $600 million in premium payments, on the basis of necessity. It also voted for the $10,000 ceiling on new homes. In the subsequent conference between the two chambers the premium payment issue was compromised at a total of $400 million, and the House agreed to accept the ceiling level. The House then voted 298 to 71 in favor of the conference compromise, while the Senate gave the measure its full approval. President Truman signed the bill on May 22, and Wyatt exulted that this victory in Congress put his program into "high gear."[16]

The Senate, having saved the VEHP from emasculation, continued its support of the Administration's housing program by passing the Wagner-Ellender-Taft bill without modification, on April 15. After two days of debate, in which a few opponents attempted to delete the public housing provisions, the Senate voiced its approval without a roll vote and sent the bill to the House Committee on Banking and Currency.[17]

With the Veterans' Emergency Housing Program in operation and the W-E-T bill approved by the Senate, it seemed that the Truman Administration's housing program would gain full congressional approval. Favor for the program had reached its zenith, however, for the conservative coalition in Congress now launched a counterattack and forced through Congress a weakened price-control bill that allowed for an across-the-board increase of 20 per cent in house prices and rents. At the suggestion of Chester Bowles, director of the Office of Price Administration, Truman vetoed the bill, although he knew that this action would end all controls. Truman told a nationwide radio audience that Congress had given him "a choice between inflation with a statute and inflation without one."[18] Because prices and rent controls formed the foundation of the VEHP, Wyatt informed the nation over CBS radio, "the veterans' housing program in its present form will be doomed unless sensible, workable price controls are put back into effect, and quickly. This is of the greatest urgency." With prices soaring and an angry veteran-consumer public at its heels, Congress realized it had been outmaneuvered; it quickly enacted an acceptable control bill. Truman signed it on July 25, thus ending twenty-five days of decontrol. Although rents and prices on construction materials returned to their original level, the hiatus dealt the VEHP a telling blow and also warned of the possibility of more severe challenges in the immediate future.[19]

In the same week of Truman's triumph in his struggle over the OPA the House Banking and Currency Committee dealt him a serious defeat by killing the Wagner-Ellender-Taft bill. The committee, led by Republican Jesse P. Wolcott, had been engaged in a two-month marathon filibuster to prevent the bill from being approved. The real estate lobby had a reliable friend in Wolcott. Until 1949 this bitter and resourceful foe of public housing almost singlehandedly prevented the House of Representatives from voting upon the comprehensive housing bill, which he viewed as a dangerous piece of socialistic legislation. The fifty-two-year-old lawyer from Port Huron, Michigan, had represented the safe Republican Sixth District since 1931. His economic conservatism came naturally: He was a direct descendant of William Bradford, the first governor of Massachusetts Bay Colony, and of Henry Wolcott, who arrived in Salem in 1636. Throughout the 1930's Wolcott had severely criticized the New Deal; he had attacked the Agricultural Adjustment Administration and the Fair Labor Standards Act with special virulence, although he voted for many other New Deal measures, including the National Industrial Recovery Act, the Works Progress Act, and the Social Security Act. In 1937 he had voted for the Wagner Housing Act, but only because it was presented as primarily a necessary economic measure. In 1938, because of the small number of Republicans in the House, Wolcott became the ranking Republican on the Banking and Currency Committee.[20] In the postwar years he used the power of this position to curtail New Deal experimentation and welfare programs that he judged as undesirable.

In order to prevent what he called "the obnoxious provision of the Wagner-Ellender-Taft Bill" from becoming law, Wolcott launched a series of delaying tactics in the Committee on Banking and Currency. With the support of ten fellow Republicans and five Southern Democrats he held the bill in a viselike grip. Although the committee had the bill for over two months, formal hearings were never held because Wolcott and his supporters, by use of parliamentary legerdemain, prevented their being called. "There's no hurry on the bill," he told newsmen. "As a matter of fact, there is a question as to the need for it at all."[21] When Chairman Brent Spence (Dem., Ky.) attempted to hold hearings, Wolcott and his supporters argued that hearings could not be held while the House was in session or without a quorum. Although these limitations were indeed legal, they had rarely been used in the long history of the Congress. Twice the committee refused to allow Robert A. Taft to testify, because

the House was in session at the time.[22] To delay the proceedings further, Wolcott presented his own housing bill in
mid-June. This bill, clearly, was not an earnest effort to get
a workable housing bill, but a stalling device. It contained
only the provision for governmental insurance of investments
for builders of rental housing and ignored all the other provisions contained in the W-E-T bill. Whenever Spence tried
to hold hearings, Wolcott demanded that his bill receive first
attention.[23]

While Wolcott was engaged in his delaying tactics, the
Truman Administration was preoccupied with the restoration
of price controls. Late in July, however, the Administration
turned to the Wagner-Ellender-Taft bill and attempted to get
it out of the Banking and Currency Committee and onto the
House floor, where speedy passage was virtually certain.
Wilson Wyatt had devoted much time in support of the bill;
he believed it would "fill in the gaps in the Veterans'
Emergency Housing Program."[24] As Congress approached
adjournment, Truman used the prestige of his office in an
attempt to dislodge the bill from Wolcott's clutches. He sent
three letters to the leaders in Congress, reminding them of
the importance he attached to the bill. "I urge upon you and
your committee the earliest possible action on S. 1952 which
is essential to the overall housing program," he wrote Spence.
"Time is of the essence."[25] But this and similar letters to
Speaker Sam Rayburn and Majority Leader John Mc-
Cormack,[26] coupled with a press release, failed to impress
Wolcott and his followers. The bill died quietly on July 31 in
an executive session of the committee. Spence, who favored
the bill, did not force it to a vote, because five Democrats
had told him privately that they would vote against it. Because he feared that an adverse vote would hurt the bill's
chances in the next session, Spence allowed Wolcott to triumph without a challenge. The unofficial vote against re-
porting the bill to the House floor was 12 to 10, with six
Republicans and five Democrats joining Wolcott.[27]

As a final ironic twist, the opponents of the bill reported that they had voted against the bill because the committee had been unable to give it the exhaustive study such controversial legislation required. Actually, hearings need not have been held, since the bill had been previously examined by the Senate Banking and Currency Committee. *Headlines* praised the House committee's decision as true democratic action: "We are gratified for the fairness of the House Banking and Currency Committee members who upheld American traditions by refusing to act on this bill without hearing the views of citizen groups affected by it."[28]

Nevertheless, Congress had not killed the Veterans' Emergency Housing Program, and by mid-summer it was in full operation. Housing Expediter Wyatt had not waited for congressional approval of his program, but had used his temporary war powers to launch it. On March 26, even before the seventy-one regional expediter offices had opened, he ordered that most "nonessential" building be halted so that scarce construction materials could be diverted into housing for veterans.[29] Wyatt believed that his greatest difficulty would be in getting materials to the local builders. Yet, the Expediter neglected to deal with a problem equally as great —the disorganization in the home-building field. The so-called construction "industry" was not in any sense of the word an industry but a potpourri of 31,000 contractors and 187,000 subcontractors whose local operations were ensnarled in a "fantastic complexity of local building codes, union regulations, price and market agreements, and ancient and self-imposed taboos."[30] Because most of these home builders were small, individual operators, few could afford to launch large-scale projects. The VEHP also encountered continual labor disputes, which, in one manner or another, prevented a steady flow of materials. Especially damaging were the lumber, steel, railroad, and coal strikes that occurred during the first fifteen months after the war.[31]

Despite such obstacles, throughout the summer and autumn

Wyatt optimistically reported new gains and predicted that the year's goal of 1,200,000 "starts" would be reached. Wyatt's monthly reports, however, were deceptive: "Starts" were not completions, and, as weeks passed, the veteran could find few of the new homes that the Housing Expediter effervescently reported. Throughout the nation there stood abandoned foundations and half-completed shells as builders waited for materials. A shortage of plywood, lath, gypsum board, electrical wiring, brass pipe, and, of all things, nails hamstrung operations.[32]

The continuing housing shortage gave the real estate lobby an opportunity to gain wider acceptance for its position. Arguing that only the removal of controls would solve the shortage, the lobby flooded the White House and Congress with telegrams and mail, while the nation's newspapers duly reported the steady stream of news releases and speeches by leaders in the building field. The lobbying gained effectiveness as shortages continued into the final months of 1946.[33]

During the autumn the general public adopted a more cautious "wait-and-see" attitude toward the VEHP. The veterans, vainly looking for the many homes reported by the Expediter to be available, became critical of the program and pointed out that families could not live in houses that existed only in the Expediter's monthly report.[34] The Republican campaign slogan "Had Enough?" reflected, in part, the growing unpopularity of the much-heralded VEHP. Realizing that total construction under the program for 1946 would fall far short of the 1,200,000-unit goal, Wyatt gambled to save his program by attempting to make spectacular gains during the late months of 1946. This attempt, however, served only to create a series of personality and policy clashes within the Administration, and these culminated in the termination of the VEHP before it had reached the halfway point of the two-year existence planned for it.

Wyatt dueled first with John D. Small, chief of the Civilian Production Agency, who was a former naval officer and industrial executive. Since the inception of the VEHP Small's business-oriented philosophy had conflicted with Wyatt's use of government controls. As head of the agency that directed industrial reconversion, Small desired to end government control of industry as rapidly as possible.[35] Ever since Wyatt's order of March 26, which sharply curtailed nonhousing construction, Small had viewed the VEHP as both unnecessary and dangerous. He believed that a sharp cutback in construction of such buildings as schools, hospitals, and factories would cause the economy to become unbalanced and would lead to widespread unemployment. When Wyatt ordered a tighter restriction on industrial use of scarce materials in late August, Small refused to comply.[36] Dr. John Steelman, Snyder's successor as director of OWMR, finally decided the issue in Wyatt's favor, but the episode left Small convinced that Wyatt's ambition had affected his sense of judgment. "During the past several weeks, he has demonstrated an increasing intolerance of the views of others," Small told Clark Clifford, a White House aide; Wyatt's intolerance had reached such a point that any criticism of the VEHP was interpreted "as opposition to veterans' housing." A totally unacceptable all-or-nothing attitude, Small concluded, pervaded the Housing Expediter's thinking.[37]

Wyatt's fight with Small had its origins in his desire to divert steel and aluminum into the infant industry of factory-made houses in order to help it produce 750,000 assembly-line homes by the end of 1947. Realizing that the home-building industry, using conventional materials and methods, could not achieve the VEHP's goal of 2,700,000 homes, Wyatt had turned, in near desperation, to the new and untested prefabrication industry. In October he tried to obtain the huge Chrysler-Dodge plant in Chicago for the Lustron Company, which planned to produce an inexpensive, assembly-line steel home. When Wyatt ordered the War Assets Administration, which disposed of government war plants, to lease the plant to Lustron, WAA refused to do so because it had already leased the plant to the ill-fated Tucker Automobile Company. After an "acrimonious meeting" on October 25, in which WAA refused to revoke what it considered a legal and binding lease with Tucker, Wyatt used the power of his office and procured a compromise settlement by which Lustron and Tucker would share the huge plant.[38]

While victorious in his intra-Administration struggles with CPA and WAA, Wyatt could not successfully bring pressure to bear on George E. Allen, director of the Reconstruction Finance Corporation. A former insurance executive and an assistant to Harry Hopkins during the New Deal, Allen had been a close friend of President Truman since the 1944 campaign. He was best known in Washington circles for his funny stories and Mississippi-bred conservatism. In return for his faithful services, Truman had rewarded the rotund Southerner with the directorship of RFC.[39] Truman feared the possibility of scandal in RFC and wanted a close, personal friend whom he could trust to serve as watchdog over this multimillion-dollar government lending corporation. Fully aware of Truman's desire to prevent graft, Allen approached his new position as would a cautious small-town banker. When Wyatt requested $90 million in loans for eleven prefabrication companies, the RFC Director flatly refused, on the ground that such loans would be poor business propositions. He pointed out that Lustron, which alone sought $52 million, had no previous record of production ability and had put up only $36,000 in assets.[40]

Wyatt denounced RFC's "business-as-usual" position and hurried to the White House, with Allen not far behind. In arguing for the loans, Wyatt displayed a lack of good judgment; the "prefab" industry was barely off the planning boards and had not yet demonstrated ability to produce several hundred homes a day. Even with government loans, the prefabrication industry had yet to solve many technical production problems. The belief that the prefabrication industry would be able to deliver 750,000 homes by the end of 1947 simply ignored reality. Instead of producing 250,000 homes, as estimated by Wyatt for 1946, the industry erected less than 40,000. After a forty-five-minute discussion with the two embattled bureaucrats Truman promised to "think it over" and left the issue dangling for three weeks while Wyatt stormed and fretted.[41]

Until Truman made his decision, Wyatt had much to worry about. Just as the RFC imbroglio reached its impasse, Truman himself dealt the VEHP a mortal blow. Rocked by the Republican triumph in the congressional elections in November, which most analysts interpreted as a vote against wartime controls, Truman announced on November 9 that he was lifting all price controls except those on sugar, rice, and rents.[42] This move practically destroyed the Expediter's program, which was based upon the continuation of prewar price levels. Truman's action constituted a retreat from his original policy and a repudiation of his firm stand on OPA, taken in July. In announcing the removal of controls, he said: "I am convinced that the time has come when these controls can serve no useful purpose. I am, indeed, convinced that their further continuance would do the nation's economy more harm than good." Fully aware that his action would kill the VEHP, Truman blandly pointed out, "The removal of price ceilings on building materials will obviously necessitate a change in the approach to some of the problems in the housing program."[43]

By ending price controls on scarce materials, moderately priced housing for veterans became a lost vision. The Republican victory, however, does not appear to have been the chief motivation for the abandonment of price controls. Truman, in his Message on Reconversion on September 6, 1945, had stated his desire to end price controls as soon as possible. By this time the war had been over for fourteen months, and supply had caught up with demand in most areas. The business community, of course, was applying great pressures upon the Administration to end controls, and within the Administration Truman's two leading advisers, John W. Snyder and Dr. John Steelman, were also arguing for the abandonment of controls. Truman had called Snyder to Washington on the day he became President, and the former Missouri banker had moved rapidly to a high position in the Administration—to the Federal Loan Bank (April 17, 1945), to the Office of War Mobilization and Reconversion (July 17, 1945), and, finally, to the position of Secretary of the Treasury (June 6, 1946). As director of OWMR, Snyder had held what *The New York Times* described as a "slack and unwilling hand" on price controls.[44] Because of his Missouri small-town banker's conservatism he became the chief focal point of criticism by New Deal economists; despite the adverse criticism, however, Truman steadfastly supported his old army buddy and promoted him whenever the opportunity arose. By early 1946 Snyder had no peer within the Administration in the area of economic policy.[45] Snyder's rapid rise to the position of Secretary of the Treasury did not mean that Truman accepted all of Snyder's advice; indeed, he quite often rejected it. But Truman did enjoy Snyder's friendship and wanted to avail himself of a viewpoint different from his own.[46]

John Steelman followed Snyder's economic policy very closely. When he succeeded Snyder in the OWMR, he continued Snyder's program of rapid decontrol. Steelman, who held a doctoral degree in economics from the University of North Carolina, had left a teaching position in Alabama College for Women in 1934 to join the United States Labor Conciliation Service. He had served as a labor mediator until 1944, at which time he opened a private labor-management consulting service, but in 1945 he returned to government service as aide to Truman's Secretary of Labor, Lewis Schwellenbach. Steelman then quickly moved into the inner circle of the White House.[47] Truman was so impressed with Steelman's work that he appointed him to the directorship of OWMR when Snyder moved to the Treasury. Steelman believed that the government should interfere in the economy as little as possible. As a labor conciliator, he had spurned the idea that he had the power to enforce decisions; the government might advise or suggest, but should not restrict or order.[48]

The abrupt end of controls demonstrated Truman's desire to return to a free economy. Although he had initially committed himself to the VEHP in his enthusiastic endorsement of Wyatt's program in February, Truman knew that housing did not comprise the entire reconversion program. He now recognized that the time for the end of controls had arrived. Controls had grown increasingly unpopular since the fight over OPA during the previous summer. In most areas supply now approximated demand; in fact, many building materials were being held off the market by speculators who sensed the imminent end of controls. Their action only intensified the shortage of housing materials. Undoubtedly, Steelman and Snyder pointed out these factors to Truman. The President also realized that if he did not abolish price controls, the new Republican Congress would do so early in January.[49] The mounting criticism of the VEHP probably contributed as well to Truman's decision. Wyatt's ability to produce only promises and "starts" instead of houses and his continual squabbling with other government agencies provided Truman with additional reasons for ending controls. While Wyatt viewed the situation from his position as housing expediter, Truman had to place housing within the perspective of the entire economy. After all factors were considered—political as well as economic—Truman decided that the time had arrived to make good his pledge, given in his Reconversion Message, to end economic controls.

Wyatt, realizing that his year's labor was virtually lost, appealed to the nation for support in a radio address, but in vain. The American people were tired of hearing about "starts" and "bold, hard-hitting programs"; as far as most of them were concerned, the Housing Expediter had promised to deliver houses, but precious few were in evidence. Wyatt's warning, "In the absence of price and wage controls there is a grave danger that a substantial part of the housing construction in 1947 will be beyond the reach of the veterans' ability to pay," received an indifferent hearing.[50] In a final attempt to counter the forces that were wrecking his program the Housing Expediter submitted his program for 1947 to Truman on November 27, with the statement that if it were not approved, he would resign. This report emphasized the need for the re-establishment of price controls and for large RFC loans to the "prefab" companies.[51]

Truman realized that Wyatt's program would never be approved by the new Congress, just as he realized that the VEHP, with its wartime controls, was no longer acceptable in an economy rapidly returning to peacetime basis. The President, therefore, had no difficulty in agreeing with his jovial poker-playing friend George Allen on the matter of the Lustron loan and probably was in equal agreement with the memorandum from John Small, dated December 3: "Mr. Wyatt's recent report is so filled with inaccuracies, garbled, partial facts, unjustified inferences, and unwarranted conclusions, that it becomes a cloud of words rather than a statement to the President of the United States." Sensing revenge, Small advised, "The plan as presented cannot be accepted and Mr. Wyatt's resignation must be accepted."[52]

In the late afternoon of December 3 Truman met with Wyatt and quietly dealt the *coup de grâce* to the VEHP by announcing that he could no longer accept continued controls and that he agreed with RFC on the Lustron question. Wyatt promptly handed the President his resignation, which went into effect immediately.[53] Accepting the terse, two-sentence letter of resignation from his embittered housing chief, Truman pointed out that the VEHP had "successfully passed through the first phase" and that "the remainder of the program must now be faced within the framework of the Government's announced policy of relaxing controls."[54] Within a week Truman removed the $10,000 ceiling, announced a relaxation of rent controls, and lifted all restrictions on construction material.[55]

By the end of 1946 the Truman Administration was forced to recast its housing program in relationship to the nation's economy and to the political situation. The VEHP was scrapped because it was no longer compatible with the expanding economy or with the thinking of the American people. Wilson Wyatt was the unfortunate victim of the situation; his goal was virtually impossible to attain, and the only tools that he could use were not acceptable to a nation that wanted to return to a life freed of wartime controls. The failure of the W-E-T bill to escape the House Banking and Currency Committee demonstrated the degree of power held by the conservative coalition in Congress, and the election of a Republican Congress removed all hope for immediate passage of the bill.

Chapter V

The Year of Postponement

IN THE FEW WEEKS following the resignation of Wilson Wyatt, the Truman Administration quickly formulated a new housing program in line with the policy of price decontrol. Most noticeable in this new program was the favorable attitude taken toward the business community. Only rent control survived the abrupt scuttling of the Veterans' Emergency Housing Program. The President's endorsement of the comprehensive housing bill remained, and Truman reaffirmed his enthusiasm for it in his State of the Union Address on January 7, 1947, but he left the responsibility for securing its passage to the Republicans' strong man, Robert A. Taft. The Republican leadership, however, found itself irrevocably divided over the public housing feature of the bill and failed to meet Truman's challenge. Thus, the year 1947 proved to be one of postponement for housing. The Truman Administration, dealing with a Congress controlled by the Republicans, could not win approval of its programs without extensive bipartisan support; yet, the Republicans among themselves were unable to agree upon a single policy.

The Administration's new housing program retained its goal —a decent home for every American family—but the method of achieving this goal was drastically changed. The ultra-liberal housing expediter, Wilson Wyatt, along with his portfolio of governmental controls, was gone. Truman appointed as his successor Raymond M. Foley, an efficient but colorless housing bureaucrat.

The new housing chief had been serving as Federal Housing Administration's chief for the past two years. Previously, he had served for eleven years as director of FHA in Michigan. The fifty-seven-year-old administrator had been a journalist earlier in his career, first as city editor (1910-1913) and then as managing editor (1913-1925) of the *Pontiac Daily Press*. Until he joined FHA, Foley had served as director of the Office of Public Relations for the State of Michigan (1925-1934).[1]

Foley's quiet demeanor and his concept of the role of the federal government in housing typified the Truman Administration's endeavor to achieve *rapprochement* with the business community. While Wyatt had assumed that the housing industry had failed and that only the employment of strict federal regulations would produce favorable results, Foley praised the past record of private housing and encouraged better production in the future; while Wyatt had antagonized the real estate and construction groups, Foley openly solicited their friendship. Government controls were anathema to Foley. The government, he believed, should serve private enterprise as adviser, helper, and co-worker, but should not dictate to it.[2] It is not surprising, then, that Foley enjoyed an amicable relationship with the housing industry. After the passage of the comprehensive housing bill in 1949 the National Association of Home Builders told its members that they need not fear impending disaster, since Foley was to supervise expenditures within the $10 billion program.[3] Truman's housing chief established equally good rapport with Congress; the Republican Eightieth Congress generously boosted his salary. Time and again he received accolades from members of the opposition for his fairness and sincere interest in an impartial housing program.[4]

Foley also enjoyed an excellent relationship with his boss.

President Truman had called him to Washington in 1945 to assume the position of administrator of FHA largely because he recalled Foley's outstanding work in Detroit's housing program during the Second World War. Truman had met him in the "Motor City" while investigating war industries and had been greatly impressed by Foley's grasp of the complex problems of wartime housing.[5] Apparently, through Foley's six and a half years as head of the government's housing agency he never seriously differed in opinion with Truman; Foley, moreover, was careful never to make any decision that would not meet with approval in the White House. During his years with the National Housing Agency and with its successor, the Housing and Home Finance Agency, Foley frequently visited the President to discuss policy. When Truman appointed him to succeed Wyatt, he extended to Foley an open invitation to bring any major problem directly to him so that it could be cleared immediately and would not become bogged down among White House aides. Truman's confidence in Foley is best illustrated by his frequent reference to him as "my authority on housing."[6]

Foley held what might best be called a balanced view of the nation's housing needs. Although he placed primary emphasis upon private housing, he acknowledged that some public housing was needed. He sincerely believed that the goal of a decent home for every family could be achieved, but realized that the government would have to play an important role in meeting that end. Consequently, he pushed for a comprehensive housing program as embodied in the Taft-Ellender-Wagner bill (the names were now reversed in deference to Taft's majority leadership). "We now need a broader attack on slums, urban and rural," he declared. "We need energetic action by government at all levels. Even more we need determined action by private enterprise to reduce costs and provide homes that more Americans of moderate and low income can afford."[7] The type of governmental action that he advocated was based upon the primacy of private enterprise in housing; he rejected the idea that public housing necessarily had to be an antiprivate-enterprise program, and he worked hard to gain the confidence of private housing officials. Foley proudly, and justifiably, referred to himself as "a champion of free enterprise in housing" and continually sought methods whereby fewer persons would be beyond the reach of adequate private housing. "The chief activity of government in housing," he held, "should be to aid and stimulate private enterprise in reduction of housing cost and in attack upon its problem areas."[8]

Public housing was not "socialism" or even a threat to private housing, at least as Foley conceived its function in meeting the existing crisis. He believed that public housing was needed to provide housing for those persons who could not afford private housing, but that federal aid from other governmental activities, such as research, would substantially lower the need for public housing in future years. Foley accepted public housing only as an expedient or substitute until private housing could devise means to provide for all income groups.[9] Unlike most proponents of public housing, Foley appreciated and understood the reasons for opposition to public housing. "I think it is unfair to brand all opponents as callous and indifferent to human need," he told the National Association of Home Builders. In a speech before the National Public Housing Conference he admonished his audience that much of the opposition to public housing sprang "from a sincere fear" of federal domination of all housing. Even after the comprehensive legislation was rejected by the Eightieth Congress in 1948, he refused to become angry, although he was deeply disappointed. "We must always bear in mind that we operate in a democratic society and that it is a basic function of such a society to seek to reconcile extreme differences of points of view on basic issues," he told a disheartened meeting of public housing officials.[10]

Truman's proposal to reorganize all the government's housing offices into the streamlined Housing and Home Finance

Agency would probably have been rejected if it had not been known that Foley was to become the administrator. With the dissolution of the National Housing Agency scheduled to take place at the end of 1947, Truman wanted to co-ordinate all of the government's housing functions under a permanent and unified agency. The plan, just one part of a wholesale modernization of the government's bureaucracy accomplished during Truman's Administration, reflected Truman's earlier scheme for streamlining county government in Missouri. If the plan had been rejected, the government's housing functions would have been scattered among thirteen different offices.[11] The opposition to this plan came from the real estate lobby, which interpreted the permanent establishment of a housing agency as a deliberate move toward federal domination of housing. "It [the reorganization plan] makes permanent a war born experiment," complained Senator Harry Cain (Rep., Wash.), who emerged in 1947 as a leading spokesman for the real estate lobby.[12] The lobby also feared the possible results of joining the Public Housing Administration with the Federal Housing Administration; the administrator of such an agency would necessarily be a supporter of public housing, to the detriment of private housing interests.[13] While these were the arguments used in an attempt to defeat the plan, the main reason why the private housing group opposed it was its basic assumption—that the government had to be permanently active in the housing field. This directly implied that the private housing groups had failed and needed permanent guidance and assistance.

The procedure for reorganization was quite unusual. Truman first submitted his proposal to the Senate. If the Senate did not reject it, it would go into effect immediately, and the House of Representatives would thereby be given no opportunity to stop it. In an attempt to block the creation of a permanent agency the House Banking and Currency Committee, under the whip of Jesse Wolcott, pushed through the House a resolution urging the Senate to reject the reorganization plan, arguing that it would unite public and private housing agencies under one administration. The Senate, however, rejected the House resolution after spirited debate, by a close vote of 47 to 38.[14] Three Republicans led the defense of the plan of reorganization: Taft, Charles Tobey (N. H.), and Ralph Flanders (Vt.). Taft, in debate with Cain and Democrat Harry Byrd (Va.), bluntly pointed out the duplicity of the real estate lobby's position: It had continually called for more federal aid until now, when there was little risk involved in many real estate undertakings; at the same time, however, it adamantly opposed any governmental aid to the groups that private housing did not serve. Taft sarcastically observed, "They do not want the Government in the housing business, but they invite the Government into the housing business." Such a position, Taft concluded, was "not very reasonable."[15]

The establishment of the Housing and Home Finance Agency on a permanent basis was an important event in the history of housing reform. The decision to create a permanent agency to conduct an active governmental housing policy was the culmination of various forces working at the local, state, and national levels for over a century. The pioneering efforts of such men as Jacob Riis, Lawrence Veiller, and Robert Wagner had eventually led to the establishment of HHFA. Although it injured the prestige of the housing industry, the reorganization assured the continuation of several governmental functions upon which private housing had come to depend. The reorganization was significant, too, because it was a bipartisan move: The Truman Administration proposed it, and a Republican Senate, led by Flanders, Tobey, and Taft, approved it.[16]

The new agency was all that the Republicans granted Truman of his housing program. Congress balked on the Taft-Ellender-Wagner bill and, instead, passed a seriously weakened rent-control bill. As he had done in 1946, Truman urged the passage of the comprehensive bill because he sincerely believed it would facilitate rapid progress on all fronts of housing.[17] The T-E-W bill, however, had no chance of becoming law; the Republicans were willing to follow Taft when he proposed legislation on labor, but not when he committed heresy by sponsoring a housing bill that dripped with "socialism." All congressmen favored housing legislation—the political situation demanded it—but not all approved of legislation that included public housing. After the Senate Banking and Currency Committee passed the bill by a narrow 7-to-6 vote,[18] Taft found that the majority of his party opposed the bill. Throughout the spring and early summer he worked hard, seeking support for it, but finally decided that Jesse Wolcott's nearly absolute power in the House Banking and Currency Committee precluded any chance of the bill being passed. Confronted by the virtual assurance of a veto by the House committee and by general Republican discomfort over public housing, Taft abandoned the bill, and it never reached the Senate floor.[19] When challenged on his failure to place the bill on the Senate agenda, Taft, with his usual candor, told the Senate that he had removed the bill from his "must" list because the public housing section would prevent its passage; he did not care to waste the Senate's time on a bill that would never pass the House.[20] In 1947, consequently, the bill died without either house of Congress having an opportunity to vote upon it.

The Truman Administration, realizing that the T-E-W bill stood little chance of passing, concentrated its attention upon getting a continuation of rent controls for the following year. If a continuation was not obtained, rent would sky-rocket. Early in 1947, therefore, Truman urged Congress to extend rent controls for another year.[21] Although opposed strongly by landlords and the real estate lobby,[22] labor and most citizen groups supported the continuation so long as an acute shortage existed.[23] Aware of the public pressure for continuation and also of the Republican disapproval of it, Truman supported continuation but placed the responsibility for passage upon Republican leadership. The Republicans, in turn, realizing the political consequences of failure to pass an extension, sent a bill to the White House, in mid-June and only after much legislative maneuvering, that provided for a 15 per cent "voluntary" increase in rent if both tenant and landlord agreed. The bill also stripped from the housing expediter, whose function had been relegated to the administration of rent controls, most of his enforcement powers. Specifically, he no longer could institute criminal proceedings against violators.[24] As the bill passed the Senate in early June, Alabama's John Sparkman voiced the sentiment of the minority who had hoped for the maintenance of strong controls: "What can you do?" he said resignedly. "It's that or nothing."[25]

Truman felt as Sparkman did and seriously considered vetoing the bill as he had the price control bill the previous summer. After gauging the disposition of the Congress, however, he signed the bill. Had he exercised his veto power, the Republican Congress might have refused to pass another bill, thereby leaving Truman with full responsibility for ending all rent controls. Heeding the opinion of Housing Expediter Frank Creedon, "The bill is better than no bill at all,"[26] Truman signed it on June 29, but simultaneously unleashed a blistering criticism of the 15 per cent "voluntary" increase in rent and the removal of strong enforcement powers. "This legislation marks a step backward in our efforts to protect tenants against unjustified rent increases," he declared. "It is of deep concern that this most unsatisfactory law represents the only major action taken by the Congress at this session with regard to housing." After accusing the real estate lobby of playing a major role in weakening controls, the President charged that the lobby had "displayed a ruthless disregard for the public welfare" by conducting "brazen operations to block programs so essential to the needs of our citizens." The indignant President urged Congress to undertake an investigation of "this selfish and shortsighted group," as "nothing could be more clearly subversive of representative government" than the methods employed by the real estate lobby.[27]

With the first session of the Eightieth Congress nearing its adjournment date, July 26, certain Republicans who had opposed public housing, in an attempt to mute criticism for their failure to pass the T-E-W bill, tried to create a façade of concern for housing reform. A lack of information had prevented prompt action on housing, they declared; the issue of public housing had so beclouded the situation that a fresh investigation "from A to Z" was necessary.[28] On July 17 Jesse Wolcott introduced a resolution in the House calling for the creation of a joint congressional committee of fourteen members, which would be given an expense account of $100,000 to study all facets of the nation's housing needs.[29] Wolcott's resolution blandly ignored the work of the Taft subcommittee and the Senate hearings on the W-E-T bill.[30] This last-minute action, a deliberate cover-up for the procrastinations of the Eightieth Congress, passed both houses without a dissenting vote.

The proponents of the T-E-W bill severely criticized Wolcott's hypocrisy. In 1946 he had filibustered against holding hearings upon the Wagner-Ellender-Taft bill; his outspoken opposition to its 1947 version had helped prevent its passage in the Senate; and now he piously called for an investigation that would cost $100,000! Democrat Adolph Sabath, eighty-one-year-old urban liberal from Illinois who two years later was to distinguish himself as a fighter for housing by engaging an opponent of the Administration's bill in a round of fisticuffs on the House floor, led the criticism by pointing out the true purpose of the resolution. It would give the veterans another round of verbiage when they needed homes; it would create an illusion of concern for good housing legislation when its aim was just the opposite; and, finally, it would postpone any action until March 15, 1948, when the committee was to report its findings. Obviously, Sabath

charged, certain Republican leaders were "influenced by one
of the rottenest and most powerful lobbies that has ever in-
fested Washington."[31]

Robert F. Wagner, now in the midst of the long illness that
prevented him from visiting Washington until 1949, released
a scathing criticism of the creation of the joint committee:

> Domestic treason is being perpetrated on the American
> Veteran and their fellow citizens by the money-mad
> real estate lobby and their unholy representatives in
> Congress. These economic vultures have not only pre-
> vented the Government from carrying out a necessary
> and comprehensive housing program but have succeeded
> in destroying an effective rent control program.

Instead of positive legislation, he charged, the Republicans
"could only come up with another housing investigation";
anybody with common sense could readily see that a housing shortage existed.[32]

The creation of the joint committee served no useful purpose; it merely postponed legislative action on housing until
March, 1948. While it provided Truman with ammunition for
the 1948 campaign, for the veterans and other homeseekers
it meant an avalanche of words and statistics but no construction. The most serious consequence of the joint committee's creation came quite by happenstance; it gave the
freshman Senator from Wisconsin, Joseph R. McCarthy, his
first real opportunity to get his name on the front pages of
the newspapers. The brash young Senator had hit upon housing as the best issue by which he could quickly gain national
prominence for himself.[33] He had yet to discover the un-
limited possibilities of ferreting alleged Communist agents
from their government positions. At this moment, he decided,
poor housing menaced the Republic.

When the congressional committee met to organize its investigation on August 19,[34] McCarthy secured the passage of
a ruling that disallowed all absentee votes. The proxies would

have awarded the committee chairmanship to liberal Republican Charles Tobey, who was already a strong supporter of the T-E-W bill. The refusal to recognize proxies, although legal, ignored procedure traditional in a legislative committee. With four proxies for Tobey rejected,[35] the committee elected Congressman Ralph A. Gamble (Rep., N. Y.), who was outspoken against public housing, as chairman and McCarthy as vice-chairman.[36] At the end of the meeting Tobey seethed with anger. He flatly accused McCarthy of bad faith and duplicity. "A sinister group," in carrying out its instructions from the real estate lobby, had engineered the coup in order to insulate the committee from the "dangers" of public housing, Tobey told the press.[37] McCarthy, unruffled by Tobey's out-of-character explosion, retorted, "I frankly didn't want Tobey to be chairman," and added, in a gross distortion of the truth, "He thinks the sole answer is public housing."[38] Upon learning of McCarthy's handiwork, Robert Wagner charged that the action not only offended congressional tradition, but was "not even in accordance with the ordinary rules of human decency."[39]

At the first hearing of the joint committee on September 10, 1947, the Vice-Chairman wrested control of the committee from Gamble, who willingly relinquished it, and for the next six months wrung all possible publicity from the investigation. "Progress reports" appeared periodically, and on occasions McCarthy made vicious, news-making attacks upon labor witnesses. In his role as vice-chairman of the committee he underwent an apprenticeship as self-appointed inquisitor, developing the sledge-hammer techniques that he later used so effectively while seeking to exhume Communist conspirators from the depths of the State Department.[40]

McCarthy worked hard to find a way to end public housing. He frequently belabored witnesses with his idea of providing state-controlled cash subsidies to low-income families as a substitute for public housing. He continually sought evidence to support his contention that public housing did not serve low-income families as much as it served families who could afford to pay normal rents. When the former public housing commissioner, Philip Klutznick, testified at a hearing in Chicago, McCarthy left the room and returned only after Klutznick had finished his testimony. Apparently, McCarthy did not want to tangle with a person well-versed in the intricacies of public housing.[41]

Despite McCarthy's antics the committee gathered considerable new information in its nationwide investigation; yet, when the committee reduced its mountain of evidence into specific recommendations, it followed the T-E-W bill very closely. The report listed eighteen proposals, including 500,000 units of public housing, expansion of FHA loan activities, slum clearance directed by local authorities, and the adoption of a national housing policy. The new features concerned an expansion of apprentice training (an abortive VEHP proposal), special housing aids for paralyzed veterans, and the elimination of restrictive practices by contractors and material manufacturers. Thirteen members of the joint committee signed this report and submitted it to Congress on March 15, 1948.[42] The one committee member who refused to sign the report was McCarthy. He did not agree with the policy of public housing, and, in one last attempt to obtain all the publicity he could from the housing issue, he submitted a minority report, entitled "Individual Views." While much of his statement agreed with the majority report, he differed on the question of public housing and reiterated his charge that public housing did not serve the low-income families as much as it did those who could afford to pay for their own housing.[43] If public housing was necessary, McCarthy concluded, it should be included in a separate bill to avoid "emotional pressures which public housing invariably arouses."[44]

McCarthy used his position not only to gain publicity for himself, but also to help fill his own depleted coffers.[45] In an involved scheme he took advantage of his membership in the Senate Banking and Currency Committee and the joint committee to milk the Lustron Corporation of $10,000. Earlier in the year, because George E. Allen had resigned from RFC, McCarthy had successfully helped Lustron obtain a loan of $37,500,000 from RFC. By no accident, he stressed the importance of further aid to prefabrication companies in his minority report on March 15, 1948. What he did not report was that at this time he was writing an article, "A Dollar's Worth of Housing for Every Dollar Spent," with the aid of a secretary in the HHFA; this article he eventually sold to Lustron for $10,000. After three publishing companies rejected the manuscript, he persuaded Carl Strandlund, president of Lustron, to buy the article, although it was not in publishable form. The purchase of this article, which cost Lustron exactly $1.43 per word, was made in such haste that Strandlund did not have time to consult his publicity department or staff members. In effect, Lustron paid McCarthy with the money it had received from RFC, since it had not yet begun full-scale production.

Senator Thomas Hennings (Dem., Mo.), in his investigation of McCarthy's activities in 1952, couched his findings in a question:

> How can Senator McCarthy justify acceptance of a $10,000 fee from Lustron, which in effect, was a fee being paid out of public funds, at a time when Lustron's continued operations and financing depended entirely upon the RFC, and which Agency, in turn, was dependent upon the Congress, and more particularly, the Banking and Currency Committee, of which he was a member, for its continued authority and operation? Did Senator McCarthy take advantage of Lustron's sensitive position and its need for continued government financing to induce its president, Carl Strandlund, to pay a fee, set by him at $10,000, for a manuscript which was neither finished or in publishable form, without any prior consultation with Lustron's public relations or executive staff and without notification to the RFC?[46]

Hennings raised some interesting questions also about Mc-Carthy's activities with a builder in Columbus, Ohio. Twice during the course of the joint committee's existence, McCarthy flew to Columbus to speak at promotional dinners for the Byers Homes Project, for which President Robert Byers paid him $500 plus expenses on each occasion. On page 5 of his "Individual Views" he reported, with all pretensions of objectivity: "The main outstanding example of what a builder of conventional houses can do was found in Columbus, Ohio, where very attractive Veterans houses are being built in sizable quantities to be sold at approximately $4,000."[47]

By 1948 the enthusiasm of urban liberals and others deeply concerned with housing had been much dampened. To be certain, houses were being built—almost 850,000 in 1947[48]—but the need of low-income families for housing continued. Although another government committee had recommended public housing, the conservative coalition in the House of Representatives precluded hopes for the enactment of suitable legislation.

During the year of postponement the establishment of the Housing and Home Finance Agency stands out as the major achievement. Its permanent status provided the machinery for future victories and for the development of long-range policy. The first administrator of this agency, Raymond Foley, reflected Truman's desire to gain the confidence of the private housing leaders. In accordance with the position he took in his Reconversion Message, Truman encouraged private housing to do as much as possible. By appointing Foley to head the housing administration, Truman gained the confidence of the industry that his Administration would not attempt to do anything to usurp the industry's position. The creation of a permanent agency, however, demonstrated Truman's belief also that the government would have to play an active role in housing for a long time to come.

Chapter VI

The Seeds of Victory

B Y THE SUMMER of 1948 it seemed that the party of Franklin D. Roosevelt had disintegrated. When Harry S Truman approached the microphones in Philadelphia Convention Hall in the early hours of July 15, 1948, to accept the nomination few Democrats wanted him to have, many people believed that the days of Democratic dominance were near an end. The party had been rocked by the formation of the Progressive party by dissident leftwing Democrats under the leadership of Henry Wallace six months earlier, and during the convention several delegations from southern states had walked out in protest against a strong civil rights platform. A "dump Truman" movement, led by two of Roosevelt's sons, Franklin D., Jr., and Elliott, had fizzled only because no suitable replacement could be found. Three weeks earlier, a confident Republican convention had nominated Thomas E. Dewey and Earl Warren to head the party's ticket, and Truman's defeat in the campaign for the Presidency seemed almost inevitable.[1]

The speech that Truman delivered to that hot, tired, and discouraged convention, however, changed the political situation. The fighting posture of the address revived the party's fainting morale, awakened the nation to Truman's program, and put the nearly prostrate party back into the battle.[2] The high point of the most important speech of the entire campaign was Truman's call for a special session of Congress; he wanted "to prove to the people whether the Republican platform really meant anything or not."[3] The confident Republicans dismissed this maneuver as a desperate gamble by a politician who saw the inevitability of impending defeat. "Mr. Truman's decision is so palpably partisan that we think it condemns itself," the *Wall Street Journal* sneered;[4] Republican Senator Arthur Vandenberg dismissed the move as "the last hysterical gasp of an expiring administration."[5]

The rousing speech, however, was not a last-minute attempt to reverse a trend toward Republican victory, but the logical extension of the general campaign strategy that Truman had developed several months earlier. Truman had never doubted that he would win; he knew the Democrats outnumbered the Republicans three to two. All he needed to do was to get the Democrats to the polls in November. "I want to say to you at this time that during the next four years there will be a Democrat in the White House," he told a group of Young Democrats in mid-May. "And, you are looking at him."[6] Truman's campaign plan was ingenious in its simplicity; he strove merely to retain the support of the hard core of the Roosevelt coalition—labor, low-income, and minority groups. Truman decided that the discussion of a few basic "bread-and-butter" issues would be the most effective way to maintain this vital support. Consequently, he sought to accomplish three things in his campaign: to focus public attention upon the reform program of the New Deal and upon his own attempts to continue it, especially in the areas of housing, labor, price control, and farm supports; to connect all Republicans with the ultraconservatives in the GOP; and to draw attention from the excellent Republican record on foreign affairs and to the party's less impressive record on domestic affairs. Truman, however, believed that foreign policy should be nonpartisan and should not become an issue in a presidential campaign. Debate over foreign policy, he believed, would do irreparable damage to the nation's world position.[7]

Because of the emphasis upon domestic welfare programs, housing figured prominently in the campaign. It had large appeal in the urban areas, and labor and veterans' organizations had supported it. The obstructionist activities of the conservative Republican leadership in the House of Representatives gave Truman a clear-cut example of how the Republicans served "the special interests." Early in 1948, Truman carefully began to build his image as the champion of housing legislation. As Congress debated the comprehensive housing bill, which he had supported since the autumn of 1945, he shrewdly manipulated the issue to his own political advantage.

In his State of the Union Message on January 7, 1948, Truman delivered what amounted to the first speech of the 1948 election campaign. The message was more a partisan polemic than a report to the Congress and the nation. Truman requested a large assortment of welfare and reform programs that surpassed in scope even those of his reconversion message. "There's something in it for everybody," the *Philadelphia Inquirer* remarked. "Truman leaves out practically nothing but the Beatitudes and the Ten Commandments."[8] The speech obviously intended to invoke the magic names of Franklin D. Roosevelt and the New Deal on behalf of Harry Truman. Truman based his message upon the assumptions that every citizen has an inherent right to certain services and that the federal government has the responsibility to see that he gets them. "We do believe that governments are created to serve the people and that economic systems exist to minister to their wants. We have a profound devotion to the welfare and rights of the individual as a human being."[9]

Believing that decent housing was such a right, Truman devoted much attention to this reform measure during the first six months of 1948. He closely associated himself with the Taft-Ellender-Wagner bill; otherwise, he feared that it might become known as the "Taft bill" instead of an Administration program.[10] Because Taft had a good chance of receiving the Republican nomination, Truman took the initiative in his State of the Union Message and continued to emphasize housing throughout the year. He realized that the conservative coalition would most likely defeat the bill again, but he believed a full-scale effort would reap untold political returns. If the Congress should pass the bill, he would have an important legislative triumph to take to the voters; if not, he could blame the Republicans.

By the time the Joint Committee on Housing issued its report on March 15, Truman had clearly established himself as the national leader of housing reform. As already mentioned, he had included housing among his potpourri of reforms in his State of the Union Message. On February 23 he sent a special housing message to Congress, in which he declared, "We have a national responsibility to assure that decent housing is available to all our people." He then spelled out a five-point program that included the continuation of rent controls, the stimulation of rental housing construction, the reduction of building costs, a half-million units of public housing, and a large slum clearance program.[11] Four days later Truman sent a long telegram from his vacation headquarters in Key West to a Washington meeting of the Veterans' Housing Conference, which Congressmen Jacob Javits and John F. Kennedy had organized to prod Congress into action. In this telegram Truman introduced his campaign theme of congressional responsibility. "The issue is now clear," Truman said. "The Congress has it within its power to follow the recommendations of the powerful real estate lobby and thus strangle the Administration's program; or it can safeguard the needs of Veterans and all low income citizens by prompt action."[12]

During the early months of 1948 the annual struggle over rent controls began anew. The present bill, which allowed for a general national rent increase of 6 per cent,[13] would expire on March 31, and Truman urged another extension. The Republican Congress, torn between the appeals of the veterans and of the real estate lobby and between the political consequences of removing controls and of commitment to a free economy, eventually passed a new bill that provided for a year's extension, but it contained a new provision to placate the landlords, which was devised by Jesse Wolcott. The bill called for the creation of local "decontrol boards" that would determine whether the local housing supply justified the continuation of controls. These local boards would have the power to end or continue controls.[14] Although the boards were supposed to be composed of all interested groups, including tenants, it was the intention of the real estate lobby to dominate the boards. The bill also continued provision for the 15 per cent "voluntary" increase in rents, but this increase could be made only if one had not been allowed during the previous year. Truman recognized this bill as the best the Congress would give him, and he signed it on March 30, but took the opportunity to emphasize how the Republican Congress had followed the wishes of the real estate lobby and had failed to protect tenants by passing "a law with teeth in it."[15]

After the joint committee filed its report, which in effect endorsed the Taft-Ellender-Wagner bill, the three senators reintroduced the bill in the Senate.[16] On April 7 the Senate Banking and Currency Committee reported the bill favorably by a 7-to-6 vote. Republicans Charles Tobey and Ralph Flanders joined five Democrats in support of the bill, while Democrat Willis Robertson (Va.) voted against it, along with five Republicans.[17] On the Senate floor, Robert A. Taft led the debate and skillfully parried the thrusts of criticism from his fellow Republicans.[18] On April 22 the Senate passed the bill by acclamation,[19] and it then went to the House Banking and Currency Committee, where Jesse Wolcott waited with his collection of obstructionist devices.

Regardless of what the House did on housing, Truman wanted to benefit politically from its action. This he emphasized in a memorandum to Raymond M. Foley, administrator of the Housing and Home Finance Agency. "We must make every effort now to see that the House passes an equally good bill," he said. "I know that we face strong opposition; but, if the legislation should fail, we must at least be sure that the responsibility for its failure is placed where it belongs."[20]

As the House committee began its study of the bill, Truman intensified his criticism of the Republican leadership. Unfortunately for Republican presidential hopes, Wolcott represented a "safe" Republican district in Michigan and had no reason to fear voter repercussion in November. In mid-May Truman remarked in an informal speech, "I just wonder how the Republican Party is going to the country on rent control and housing."[21] During Truman's "nonpolitical" trip to the Far West in June the conservative Republican leadership in the House defeated the T-E-W bill, enabling Truman to document his charges of the present Congress being "the worst" Congress. Republican Jesse Wolcott could not have helped Truman's political fortunes more effectively if he had tried. Liberal Republicans attempted to circumvent Wolcott, but were unsuccessful. Knowing that Wolcott would try to kill the bill in committee as he had done in 1946, Republican Jacob Javits circulated a "discharge" petition that would have brought the bill directly to the House floor without the committee's approval. The petition required 218 signatures, but Javits was able to collect only 161.[22]

Meanwhile, Wolcott busied himself in writing his own housing bill. His plan to kill the bill in committee and then replace it with his own bill received a temporary setback when three Republicans on his committee joined eleven Democrats to overcome the thirteen opponents of the bill. Republican Hardie Scott (Pa.) switched his vote at the last minute to deal Wolcott a defeat,[23] but the resourceful Michigan lawyer had another weapon with which to kill the bill: the Rules Committee headed by conservative Leo Allen of Illinois. In an unusual meeting of that committee Wolcott appeared and testified against the bill reported by his own committee. Public housing, he charged, would "fashion the key to open the door to socialism in America." The committee agreed with Wolcott and refused by a vote of 6 to 2 to allow the bill to reach the House floor.[24] For the third consecutive year the House of Representatives was not given the opportunity to vote on the comprehensive housing bill. Now that "socialism" had been routed successfully, Wolcott promptly called a meeting of his committee to consider his own bill.

The House action embarrassed the liberal wing of the Republican party, which had definite plans for capturing the White House. Even the supposedly conservative Taft could not persuade his fellow Republicans to pass the T-E-W bill. Wolcott, assisted by Leo Allen, Speaker Joe Martin, and Whip Charles Halleck, presented a united front against it.[25] As Senator Flanders recalls in his memoirs: "House sentiment was strongly against public housing. Taft was determined in his support for this. There is in my memory a clear picture of Taft backing Joe Martin up against the wall of the Senate chamber and demanding in no uncertain terms that the House accept the bill."[26]

In early June, with the T-E-W bill in the House committee, Truman headed westward on his "nonpolitical" train junket, ostensibly to accept an honorary degree from the University of California. This trip, however, was a key factor in Truman's political strategy. When he began the journey, his popularity had supposedly reached a very low point, and he needed to revive the Democratic party's faith in his chances in November.[27] On this trip, which amounted to

his first "whistle-stop" tour of the campaign, Truman un-
veiled his off-the-cuff speaking technique and in seventy-one
short, folksy talks from the rear platform of his train criticized
the domestic record of the Eightieth Congress: In January
he had given the Congress a program; it had balked, and
now he had to go directly to "the people" and tell them "the
facts."[28]

The trip coincided neatly with the House action on housing,
which enabled Truman to document his charges against "the
worst" Congress with headlines from the front pages of the
newspapers. The Republicans, he said, refused to allow the
House to vote on his housing bill "because they are afraid if
it is submitted to a vote it will pass."[29] When the Rules
Committee killed the housing bill, Truman told an audience
in Indianapolis that although this action was "tragic," it was
only typical of this "special interest" Congress.[30] Out of this
discussion on housing and other domestic issues emerged Truman's basic campaign theme: The Republican party, as represented by the Eightieth Congress, served the business community, while the Democratic party, the party of Franklin
D. Roosevelt, acted in the interests of "the people."[31] In Jefferson City, Missouri, he summarized this theme: "There is
just one big issue. It is the special interests against the people.
. . . You now have a special interest Congress because only
one-third of you voted in 1946. You are getting just what you
deserve."[32] By the end of this trip Truman had completed
the first stage of his campaign. He had succeeded in focusing
public attention upon domestic affairs, and, by attacking
his opposition in its most vulnerable spot, had drawn attention
from its positive support of his drastically new foreign policy
of containment. He had developed a set of issues that placed
his Administration and the Democratic party in a favorable
light to the voting strength of the urban coalition, and he
had made the nation aware of the failure of the Eightieth
Congress to pass any of his domestic program. Thus Truman
shaped the entire structure of the campaign to his advantage.

Events during the subsequent two weeks further enhanced Truman's position. After the Rules Committee had killed the T-E-W bill, Wolcott had introduced his own bill, which provided very liberal depreciation allowances for tax purposes to builders of large rental apartment buildings and an expansion of the mortgage-insurance program of the Federal Housing Administration.[33] He then immediately called a meeting of his committee to consider the bill, at which time he refused to recognize any amendments or points of order. Rushing the bill to the House floor the next day, he introduced it under a special "gag and bind" rule, obtained from the Rules Committee, which limited debate and prohibited amendments. Despite these arbitrary methods, the bill passed, 319 to 90, primarily because it did provide some aid for construction of the much needed housing.[34] Its passage prompted Brent Spence, one of several Democrats who criticized Wolcott's highhanded methods, to remark, "Exercise of arbitrary powers anywhere in a republic by the elected officials is more dangerous than socialism."[35] Wolcott had triumphed again, but so had Harry Truman.

The Senate, irritated by Wolcott's flagrant use of power, refused to hold a conference to reconcile the differences between its T-E-W bill and Wolcott's bill. Allen J. Ellender denounced Wolcott as "a little czar," while Republican Charles Tobey charged that the bill was "a snare and a delusion," a "fake housing bill," and a "monstrosity put out to deceive the American people."[36]

This congressional action occurred within the shadow of the Republican convention, which opened in Philadelphia on June 21. The disagreement over housing between Taft and Wolcott created platform problems for the Republicans. "It seems that they outsmarted themselves and will have no housing bill whatsoever, much to the dismay of the Republican platform writers in Philadelphia," wrote Congressman Mike Monroney (Dem., Okla.) to Raymond Foley shortly after Wolcott had won his personal war against "socialism."[37] The Republican platform attempted to straddle the breach by affirming the goal of a decent house for all citizens, but, in a carefully guarded phrase, stated that private enterprise should provide the housing; federal funds should be used for public housing and slum clearance "only where there is a need which cannot be met either by private enterprise or by states and localities."[38] The Republican platform, therefore, cautiously endorsed the basic principles in the Taft-Ellender-Wagner bill. One question remained, however: Who would decide when federal aid was needed, a Taft or a Wolcott? This Harry Truman set out to determine.

The Republican nominee, New York's Governor Thomas E. Dewey, had never stated his position on public housing and slum clearance. Fully aware of the split within his party on this subject, he decided to remain uncommitted, thereby hoping to avoid further factionalism during the campaign.[39] In his acceptance speech, which set the tone of his campaign, Dewey refrained from making any specific commitments, but instead issued a call for national unity. His attitude only encouraged Truman's plan of dwelling upon the domestic record of the Eightieth Congress. Dewey's acceptance speech sounded more like an inaugural address:

> Our people yearn to move to a higher ground, to find a common purpose in the fine things which unite us. The unity we seek is more than material. . . . Spiritually, we have yet to find the means to put together the world now broken in pieces, to bind up its wounds, to make a good society, a community of men of good will that fits our dream.[40]

Despite the actions of some members of his own party on housing, Dewey could have discredited Truman's self-created position as an earnest supporter of housing by discussing the Wilson Wyatt episode. But, by taking the "high road," Dewey allowed Truman to discuss only the issues that would best serve the Democratic party.

When the Republicans ended their convention, they were confident of victory; after all, the opponent was a political accident who was leading a badly divided party, not the invincible Roosevelt and his powerful coalition. Even Taft, the unsuccessful, disheartened candidate for the Republicans' nomination, assumed that Dewey would win: "I feel confident that the new Administration will advance the principles in which you and I believe," he wrote to a supporter in Missouri shortly after the convention.[41] But the unresolved split within the Republican party on such welfare issues as housing was to be an Achilles' heel.

Just before Congress adjourned for the Republican conclave, it had passed a housing bill sponsored by Republican Senator William Jenner of Indiana.[42] This bill provided governmental insurance for veterans' cooperative housing developments and RFC purchase of second mortgages on veterans' homes. With the exception of rent control and the creation of HHFA, the bill represented the sum total of the action on housing by the Eightieth Congress. The provisions of the Jenner bill paled in comparison even with the Wolcott bill.

Truman waited until after the conclusion of the Republican convention before he commented on the bill. On July 1 he signed Jenner's bill, calling it the "teeny-weeny" housing bill because it provided only limited assistance for veterans' housing. In his remarks he condemned it as "hasty patchwork" and "slipshod legislation" and pointed out that the Congress had failed to provide any of the five points he had requested on February 23. The responsibility for this poor record fell upon the Republican leadership, he charged.[43] Significantly, Truman failed to distinguish between Dewey, Taft, or Wolcott in his indictment of the opposition; until November he regarded all Republicans as identical with the conservatives in the House of Representatives. "The failure to pass decent housing legislation is a sad disappointment to the millions of our people who are so desperately in need of homes," Truman pointed out. "We cannot accept as final a decision reached by such undemocratic methods." He concluded his attack by returning to his basic campaign theme: "This is one of the many jobs left unfinished by the Eightieth Congress."[44]

By the time the Democrats assembled in Philadelphia on July 12 Truman had made the foundation for a successful campaign, but this spadework went unnoticed. Most party regulars were either in a state of panic or resigned to defeat. Truman's political advisers, especially White House aide Charles S. Murphy, believed that the party needed a dramatic maneuver by the President to dispel the defeatism that permeated its rank and file. An unsigned memorandum, dated June 29, set forth a plan to revive the party's enthusiasm. Although the authorship is unknown, the arguments were primarily Murphy's. "This election can only be won by bold and daring steps, calculated to reverse the powerful trend now running against us," the memorandum stated. The only question was how to do this. "The boldest and most popular step the President could possibly make would be to call a special session of Congress early in August."[45] A special session, the memorandum continued, would afford Truman several political advantages. It would provide further evidence of the disparity between the Republican platform and its record in Congress; it would focus attention upon the conservative wing of the Republican party and away from Dewey; and, ultimately, it would force Dewey either to accept or to denounce the Eightieth Congress. On the housing question, it would make public the split between the Wolcott and Taft supporters and would compel Dewey to take a position with one of them.[46] Thus, in essence, the call for a special session would dramatically crystallize the issues that Truman had been carefully developing since January and would publicize the "rotten record" of the Congress and the "Neanderthal men" who dominated it.

This idea of a special session was not original with the author of the memorandum, for several persons had already suggested it.[47] Taft had curtly dismissed such a possibility when asked by reporters: "I can't see any reason for it."[48] Even Truman was inclined against calling such a session, as late as July 2. In answer to a St. Louis congressman who had urged such a move in order to get the housing bill passed, Truman wrote: "I can't see very well the necessity for calling back that same Congress to do nothing about it [housing] although I have the matter under serious consideration."[49] Within a few days, however, when Samuel I. Rosenman began to draft the acceptance speech, Truman had decided that the party's attitude of defeatism required a dramatic move. "The Democratic Party was dispirited and dejected. I meant to give them something to cheer about and something to campaign for," Truman recalls in his *Memoirs*.[50]

He more than accomplished his purpose, for his speech roused the convention and lifted the gloom that pervaded Convention Hall.[51] Addressing the delegates, Truman said:

> Now the Republicans came here a few weeks ago and they wrote up a platform. I hope you all have read that platform. . . . They promised to do in that platform a lot of things that I have been asking them to do, and they had refused to do when they had the power. . . . The Republican platform comes out for slum clearance and low rental housing. I have been trying to get them to pass this housing bill ever since they met the first time and it is still resting in the Rules Committee.

As the convention delegates cheered his remarks, Truman continued to outline the disparity between the Republican platform and congressional performance on several domestic issues. Finally, he brought the delegates to their feet, applauding excitedly, when he informed them:

> I am going to call that Congress back and I am going to ask them to pass laws halting rising prices and to meet the housing crisis, which they say they are for in their

platform. Now my friends, if there is any reality behind
the Republican platform, we ought to get some action
out of the short session of the Eightieth Congress, and
they could do this job in fifteen days if they wanted
to do it.

As Truman told the enthusiastic convention, "What that
worst Eightieth Congress does in this special session will be
the test. The American people will decide on the record."[52]

This speech, in view of the subsequent campaign, was the
turning point in the election. By calling Congress back into
the midsummer heat of Washington, Truman turned attention
upon domestic concerns and away from foreign affairs. He
succeeded in equating the Republican party with its leadership in the House, a fallacious connection that Dewey never
attempted to correct. Although aware that he had a struggle
before him, Truman did not view himself as a desperate
candidate, grasping at any method to achieve victory. The
special session, although not planned long in advance, nonetheless fitted into the general strategy that Truman had followed since early in the year; his move was merely an advanced phase of his attempt to focus attention upon a few
issues, such as housing, which would best serve his political
aims.

Chapter VII

Truman's Finest Hour

SELDOM had the outcome of an American presidential election seemed so certain as the one in 1948. No knowledgeable political observer believed Harry S Truman could defeat New York's Governor Thomas E. Dewey. Not only did Dewey and his "team" provide formidable opposition, but the Democratic party had suffered damaging secessions by the Wallace Progressives and the Dixiecrats. Truman's acceptance speech before the Democratic convention in mid-July had injected some hope into his party, but his candidacy evoked little genuine enthusiasm, and many party regulars were conspicuously absent throughout the campaign. George Gallup found few dissenters when he predicted that Truman would receive no more than 44 per cent of the popular vote, and Elmo Roper stopped taking voter samples in mid-September, so certain was he that Dewey would win.[1]

Truman, however, never doubted that he could win,[2] but he realized that an extensive campaign would be necessary in order to retain the support of the hard core of the Roosevelt coalition, composed primarily of labor, minority, and low-income groups.[3] Since he had presented his imposing array of reforms and welfare programs to Congress in January, Truman had cultivated certain issues through which he believed he could achieve this end. The emphasis upon domestic policies had led to an unexpected attack on the Republican Eightieth Congress during his "nonpolitical" trip in June. The failure to secure passage of these programs, coupled with the criticism of the "do-nothing" Congress, constituted the substance of his fiery acceptance speech at the convention. He also sketched for the delegates an outline of his campaign, which he developed in detail throughout the remainder of the summer and autumn.

Truman's campaign appeal was liberal in content, but conservative in purpose. By conducting an offensive campaign against the Republican Congress, he actually staged a defensive action in an attempt to retain the support of the Roosevelt coalition. His ultimate purpose was to protect the reforms of the New Deal from possible erosion or even wholesale eradication by a Republican administration.[4] During September and October he continually reminded the voters of the material gains they had derived from the New Deal, and, to emphasize this point, he frequently contrasted the prosperous year of 1948 with the depression of Herbert Hoover's Administration. "Democratic policies turned hard times into good times," he reminded his listeners.[5] In fact, Truman dwelt so frequently upon the failures of the Hoover Administration that it seemed that Hoover, not Dewey, was his opponent. Truman warned that the Republicans wanted to return to a domestic policy of "boom and bust," as followed by Harding, Coolidge, and Hoover, and that the purpose of the 1948 Republican campaign was ultimately to restore Hoover's policies and to eliminate many New Deal reforms.[6] "The Republicans don't like the New Deal. They never liked the New Deal, and they would like to get rid of it," Truman declared. The Republicans, he told an audience in Akron, were "waiting eagerly for the time when they can go ahead and do a real hatchet job on the New Deal without interference."[7] His approach rejected the idea of nationalism, as presented in Dewey's "unity" campaign theme, and emphasized the social and economic welfare of the lower and middle classes. "Think it over when you go into the voting booths next month," Truman told his audiences time and time again. "Think of the gains you've obtained in the last sixteen years—higher wages, social security, unemployment compensation, federal loans to save your homes and a thousand other things—and then think of the Tafts and Tabers."[8]

Truman knew his America well; he understood what policies appealed to the large voting blocs. When he spoke to the thousands who gathered excitedly around his train platform, he simply told them, "Vote in your own interest," and then spelled out in detail specific governmental programs that the New Deal had inaugurated to help certain disadvantaged groups and described the programs he had asked the Republican Congress to pass.[9] While Dewey talked of a rosy "unity" between labor and management or landlord and tenant, Truman talked about a "slave labor act" and rent control.

Throughout the campaign Truman purposely ignored foreign policy. He mentioned this topic in only one speech, and on this occasion he merely suggested that it should be bipartisan and divorced from politics.[10] Although he discusses his conviction in his *Memoirs*,[11] the fact does remain that Republican support for his new foreign policy of containment clearly refuted his charges against Congress as "do-nothing" and "the worst." Senator Robert A. Taft, not above playing politics, developed this line of criticism of Truman's attack upon the Republican Congress:

> The attitude of the President toward Congress is a sad contrast to the cooperation which he has received in the whole field of foreign policy. We have done our best to assist him, and sacrificed many of our own views

so that it might not appear to the world that America spoke with two voices. Yet now, the President is trying to make political capital of the policy made possible by Republicans and Congressional cooperation, while he vilifies the Congress.[12]

Candidate Dewey, however, did not pursue this line of criticism, and Truman succeeded in directing public attention toward the areas that would best serve his own interests.

Because Truman decided to concentrate upon domestic reform and welfare programs to the exclusion of foreign policy, housing played a significant role in his campaign. It substantiated his campaign theme of "the people" against "the special interests."[13] He had carefully cultivated the housing issue throughout the first six months of 1948 and had used it as one of the major reasons for calling Congress into special session. Not only did housing appeal to the groups whose support he sought, but the history of the comprehensive housing bill justified his criticism of the Congress. The Republican Congress had followed the requests of the real estate lobby (a "special interest") and had refused to pass the bill, although "the people," as represented by the President,[14] had continually urged that the bill be passed.

When Truman announced the special session to the Democratic convention, he said that the emergency in housing and the spiraling inflation had prompted his decision. He insisted that these two problems could not wait until 1949 for congressional action.[15] On July 27 he presented his message to the special session of Congress and urged that these two problems receive immediate attention; however, he also presented a long list of other measures for consideration. In calling attention to the growing problem of slums and the persistent housing shortage, he said: "I have recommended time and again that the Congress pass a comprehensive housing bill which would help us obtain more housing at lower prices, both for sale and rent. A good housing bill passed the

Senate on April 22. . . . This is the bill we need. We need it now, not a year from now."[16]

By calling a special session to reconsider the Taft-Ellender-Wagner bill, Truman placed the Republican congressional leadership in a difficult political position. The Republican platform called for a similar housing program, and Taft co-sponsored the bill, but the Republican leaders in the House of Representatives stood firmly opposed to the "socialistic" measure. Truman's bold move, therefore, exposed a division in the Republican ranks. The emphasis upon housing was, of course, merely part of Truman's campaign strategy to turn attention away from Dewey and to the clique of conservatives who dominated the House. He sought also to force Dewey either to endorse or to condemn their actions. Truman knew that the Congress would not pass the T-E-W bill, but he wanted to demonstrate to the nation that the real intentions of the Republicans belied the liberal housing platform adopted at their convention.[17]

The Republicans, trapped between their liberal platform and their conservative record, were embarrassed and angry when they assembled in Washington on "Turnip Day." The President had resorted to "cheap politics," they snarled; several even suggested adjourning Congress within minutes after the special session opened.[18] In a formal statement the majority leadership in Congress denied that either inflation or housing required emergency legislative action and denounced Truman's action as "solely a political maneuver."[19] Nevertheless, they did agree to study Truman's proposals and to take limited action on both housing and prices. Many party members believed a housing bill, designed to stimulate low-cost rental housing but bereft of any controversial provisions, should be passed. To prevent any public disagreement within the "unity" party prior to the election, the Republican hierarchy decided to prevent the T-E-W bill from reaching either floor of Congress. Taft agreed to this, but affirmed his intention to reintroduce the bill in 1949.[20]

This tacit compromise disintegrated on August 5, however, when two liberal Republican senators, who apparently placed principle above party even in an election year, rebelled against their party's leadership. In a morning meeting of the Senate Banking and Currency Committee, Chairman Charles Tobey and his fellow New Englander Ralph Flanders, with Taft sitting in the audience, voted with five Democrats to amend Jesse Wolcott's housing bill by adding provisions for public housing and slum clearance.[21] The absolute veto of the conservatives in the House and the undemocratic methods employed by these men to defeat the housing bill in June had aroused Senator Tobey's anger. He wanted to expose the dictatorial powers being wielded by the House leadership on housing legislation and had enlisted Flanders' support. Tobey and Flanders knew, of course, that the Senate had passed the T-E-W bill in April and that the House had served notice that it would not pass the measure during the special session. Nevertheless, both senators had served on the Joint Committee on Housing and had become convinced of the pressing need for the comprehensive bill. Unlike many of their fellow Republicans, they accepted Truman's position that the housing shortage did constitute an emergency situation that required immediate attention. Therefore, despite the opposition of Speaker Joe Martin, Whip Charles Halleck, and Banking Chairman Jesse Wolcott, Tobey and Flanders determined to secure the passage of some kind of housing bill or, at least, to force the House leaders to settle the matter in a conference between the two chambers during the highly publicized special session.[22]

This action placed Taft in a very uncomfortable position. He had already agreed that he would not support his bill until the next Congress, and, as a Republican leader, he wanted to avoid any intraparty fight before the election. The move by the two insurgent New Englanders, therefore, forced Taft to speak against his own bill on the Senate floor for the sake of party unity and to honor his pledge to the House Republican leaders.

After Flanders reported the amended bill to the Senate on the afternoon of August 5, Senator Joseph McCarthy, who had previously dueled with Tobey over the chairmanship of the joint committee in 1947, introduced his own housing bill in the form of an amendment to the bill reported by Flanders.[23] McCarthy's bill provided for an expanded Federal Housing Administration mortgage insurance program for builders of inexpensive houses or apartments and for an insurance program with a 2¾ per cent yield to guarantee a profit for such builders. His bill deleted public housing and slum clearance. The Senate, then, had essentially two bills before it. This situation prompted two days of heated debate, much of it between Republicans, and the proximity of the election further helped to produce a most bizarre congressional session.

When McCarthy introduced his bill, he pointed out that, since the House Rules Committee had refused to pass the T-E-W bill in June, the amended bill introduced by the Senate Banking Committee would only result in a repetition of this action. After telling the Senate that Jesse Wolcott had instructed him to inform them that public housing would never pass the labyrinth of House committees,[24] McCarthy argued that his bill would be far better than no housing bill at all.[25] This statement, which amounted to an ultimatum to the Senate to pass the McCarthy bill, caused Tobey to erupt in righteous indignation. He shouted:

> Let us find out who is controlling the interest of humanity in this country. Where has government of the people, by the people, and for the people gone if one man, the head of a powerful committee of one branch of the Congress may say, "We shall not let the people's representatives vote on public housing, slum clearance and urban rehabilitation?"[26]

Taft, caught in the middle of this party feud, reluctantly stood by his agreement with the House leadership. He did so, he said, for the sake of practicality; the House would accept McCarthy's bill, but not the one that he cosponsored, and a limited bill would be better than no bill at all. Taft assured his colleagues that he had done everything he could to persuade the House leadership to approve the T-E-W bill: "I have not changed my position. I'm for it, but this Congress cannot possibly enact it. I ask the Senate to postpone the public housing fight until January."[27] Democratic vice-presidential nominee Alben Barkley did not allow this golden moment to pass without comment, for seldom did Taft allow himself to be trapped in such an embarrassing position. "The Senator from Ohio," Barkley observed, "apparently has surrendered his position. . . . I do not myself propose to surrender my convictions."[28] Republican Tobey agreed with Barkley, and, mingling Biblical quotations with mild curses, he denounced the "oligarchy" that dominated the House: "Damn the legislative torpedoes;" he said at one point. "Let's go ahead and give the country what the American people want."[29]

The Tobey-Flanders insurrection failed, however, and twelve Republicans who had previously voted for the T-E-W bill followed their leader from Ohio and voted for McCarthy's bill. It passed by a vote of 48 to 36; eleven Democrats, nine of them Southerners, joined with thirty-seven Republicans in support of the bill, and twenty-four Democrats and twelve Republicans voted against it.[30] The next day the House, after hearing Wolcott praise the bill as one that would immediately "encourage, accelerate, and expand" inexpensive housing construction, speedily passed the bill by an overwhelming majority, 352 to 9.[31] Truman signed the bill on August 10 only because it would provide some additional aid for housing construction. He pointed out, however, that it was an "emasculated housing bill" and emphasized that "the record shows clearly where the responsibility lies for this denial of the democratic process."[32]

The action taken on housing by the special session more than fulfilled Truman's expectations. The Republican Congress had not only refused to pass the bill he had requested, thereby repudiating the Republican platform, but it had also engaged in a bitter intraparty fight. By balking, as well, on all the other programs requested by Truman, Congress justified Truman's characterization of it as "do-nothing" as far as domestic matters were concerned.[33] These events afforded Truman a variety of tactics to use in the ensuing "whistle-stop" campaign. Having clearly demonstrated the discrepancy between the Republican platform and the Republican congressmen who would have to enact it, Truman more than made his point, and he moved into the actual campaign with a well-equipped arsenal with which to make his bid to the electorate.[34]

Truman launched his campaign on Labor Day in Grand Rapids, Michigan, and ended it on election eve in his native Missouri. During this two-month-long ordeal Truman hammered away on the issues that he had carefully been developing since January. He devoted a considerable part of seventy-five speeches to housing, and used this issue to focus attention upon the Republican Congress and away from his opponent Thomas Dewey. By implication, he attempted to convey the impression that all Republicans held the same basic attitudes toward housing; he did this by never mentioning the Republican presidential candidate by name and by charging that the Republican Congress, not a certain small group, had defeated his housing bill. He never distinguished between those who supported his program and those who opposed it. When giving a speech, he would first discuss his own program with the audience, then, after emphasizing how it would have helped the local situation, he would tell them how his bill had been killed by the Republicans "at the behest of the real estate lobby." Such action, he declared, would be continued if his party were not returned to office.[35] "This housing situation is intolerable and inexcusable," he said in Buffalo, New York, to an audience of five thousand persons who had stood in a heavy rain to hear him "give 'em hell." "A rich country like ours can afford decent homes for its citizens, but still over three million families live doubled up, five million in slums."[36]

Closely related to the housing shortage was the continued existence of slums. "There is nothing more un-American than a slum," Truman told his audience at Madison, Wisconsin. "How can we expect to sell democracy to Europe until we prove that within the democratic system we can provide decent homes for our people?"[37] The housing-slum problem could have been solved, he informed an assembly gathered at Yonkers, New York, by the passage of the comprehensive bill, but, instead, "the Republican leaders, working hand in glove with the real estate lobby, stalled off action on the Federal housing bill until the last hours of the Eightieth Congress. And then they very quietly murdered that bill and passed a fake one with which to fool you people."[38] The Republicans, he continually charged, had merely served as "messenger boys" for the real estate lobby—first, when they stalled on housing in 1947 by creating a new investigation committee; second, when they passed weakened rent control bills; and third, when they allowed the Rules Committee to kill the Administration's bill in 1948. After the Eightieth Congress had "murdered" his bill, he told his audiences, the Republican convention adopted a platform that called for a bill identical to the one the Republican congressmen had killed. This action had partially prompted him to call a special session to give the Republicans an opportunity to show if they meant what their platform said. But, Truman concluded, they remained true to form and passed a "phony housing bill."[39]

Taft's action in the special session gave Truman clear evidence to cite in his charges of duplicity on the part of the

Republicans. When "Taft ran out on his own bill," Truman declared, he revealed the true intentions of the Republicans on housing.[40] Before a breakfast gathering of Democrats in Taft's Cincinnati, he further charged:

> He [Taft] tried to pose as a man who wanted decent housing legislation to wipe out slums in which millions of our veterans and other citizens are forced to live. . . . After his defeat at the Republican convention in Philadelphia, Taft didn't have to carry on his pretense of caring about the needs of the people. He could act in his real character—as a cold-hearted, cruel aristocrat.[41]

This poor record on housing, Truman explained, merely modified the Republicans' 1928 campaign slogan of "two cars in every garage"; now, he declared, it was "two families in every garage."[42]

Truman believed that the record of the Eightieth Congress on housing explained Dewey's refusal to discuss the issues. Through his theme of the "soothing syrup" of "unity," Dewey attempted to cover up the fact that the Republican Congress had followed the directions of the real estate lobby and ignored the welfare of the people.[43] Frequently, Truman underscored Dewey's refusal to explain his position on housing, as in his speech at New Haven, Connecticut:

> The Governor of the State of New York wants to be President. He was asked right at the height of the fight in Congress what he thought of the Taft-Ellender-Wagner Bill. Do you know what he said? "I haven't had time to read it." Well, he pretends to know something about housing, but if he's too busy to read the bill that would have made the difference between houses and no houses, then he doesn't know much.[44]

Even more damaging, Truman declared, was Dewey's silence during the special session: "He didn't lift a finger after he became the Republican nominee, running on the Republican platform, to get a housing bill through when I called the Special Session in July."[45] In contrast to Dewey's evasiveness, Truman had a specific program: "You know where I stand. We are just trying to find out where the other fellow stands," he reminded his audience in Cincinnati.[46]

Dewey, confident of victory, apparently decided not to rock the boat by taking a position on such a controversial issue as housing.[47] Recognizing the split within his party, he desired to avoid alienating either faction. Dewey made only one speech on housing, but his remarks only justified Truman's attacks. Dewey spoke for thirty minutes, but made only one concrete proposal—the modernization of local building codes. Speaking at the dedication of the public housing development in New York City named in honor of Al Smith, Dewey praised the local authorities for using federal funds, but he carefully refrained from saying whether he would continue such a program. Instead of delineating a program supported by specific proposals, he resorted to the recitation of a long string of lofty but empty phrases. "We will not be satisfied until the curse of slums and tenements is lifted from every American family and every American child," he declared with conviction. The speech continued in much the same nebulous vein:

> We need to cut the impenetrable underbrush of theory and disagreement and dispute and draw up a workmanlike program. We must work out not a government program or a labor program or a building program. The program we must have is one worked out by labor, industry, our lending institutions, and government, local, state, and national. It must be the kind of program that can be agreed to and that can be consistently followed. That kind of agreement is not impossible to get. With competence, firmness and real encouragement on the part of government, we can get it.

If federal aid was needed, and he did not state that it was, it would have to be distributed on "a realistic, practical basis."[48] The real "impenetrable underbrush," Dewey must have realized as he spoke, was the vacuousness of his speech; he substituted platitudes for programs, vagueness for concreteness. At the close of his campaign Dewey remarked that "Governor Warren and I have fully and frankly stated our views on the issues of the campaign."[49] If this were so, then he had no housing program whatsoever. "Unity," a bankrupt theme when applied to housing, could not match Truman's own carefully formulated program. Anyone who was familiar with the housing situation would know that the basic issues at stake in housing defied any hope for "unity."

Despite the vulnerability of his party's record on the T-E-W bill, Dewey could have effectively countered many of Truman's charges on housing. The Republican nominee never mentioned, for example, that the Democratic Congress refused to pass the same bill in 1946; he failed to criticize Truman's fumbling of the Veterans' Emergency Housing Program, which forced the resignation of Wilson Wyatt; nor did Dewey point out that many Republicans supported the T-E-W bill or that a Republican Senate passed a bill for the reorganization of the Housing and Home Finance Agency. Most important, however, was Dewey's failure to present a specific program of his own.

Dewey also neglected to challenge the many distortions and oversimplifications Truman made on housing; these Dewey should have been able to turn into a mockery. Such statements as the following were never answered by the overcautious Republican candidate: "The Republican Congress flatly refused to help the low-income families"; "Republican policies are depriving millions of families of the housing they need"; "The Republicans don't care whether the lack of housing is holding back the expansion of industry"; or "They don't care about the human suffering caused by slums."[50] Because such statements, excusable in an American political campaign, were never questioned or refuted, many persons probably decided they were correct. The closest Dewey ever came to challenging Truman's charges was, "Nobody believes that stuff, including the people who are saying it."[51] A point-by-point dissection of Truman's speeches on housing alone would have proved more effective than the evasiveness that characterized Dewey's entire campaign; it certainly could have done little harm.

Dewey's aloofness, therefore, enabled Truman to concentrate upon the issues that best served his political fortunes. More important, because Dewey refused to respond to his challenges, Truman was able to attack with impunity. The election results affirm the soundness of Truman's strategy of dwelling upon a few domestic issues; he carried the large urban areas, with the exception of traditionally Republican Cincinnati, and New York City, where Henry Wallace received half of his votes. Over 60 per cent of Truman's 2,100,000-vote plurality came from the nation's twelve largest cities; consequently, most of the states with large urban populations fell into the Democratic column.[52] Housing alone probably did not sway a large number of voters, but, coupled with the other issues of importance to the urban areas, it provided an attractive liberal package for the urban voter. On the day following the election Truman exulted, "Labor did it!"[53] A more accurate analysis might have declared that a well-rounded liberal program which appealed to both urbanites and farmers provided the formula for victory.

Chapter VIII

The High Point of Fair Deal Reform

T HERE WAS a greater significance in the 1948 Presidential campaign than the election of Harry S Truman of Independence, Missouri. To be sure, Truman's victory was a great personal triumph, for he had fought hard and bravely in what seemed to be a hopeless cause. Of greater importance, however, was that the election made permanent the reforms of the New Deal. Truman had campaigned for a program that promised to continue and to expand the New Deal and had battled against the forces he thought would return America to a government of "the special interests." He believed that his victory gave him a mandate to continue what he called "the experiment of achieving economic abundance and basic human rights in a society of free institutions and free men."[1]

The logical product of this election was Truman's Fair Deal message to Congress on January 5, 1949. Urban liberalism—the reform impulse of the factory, the tenement, and the ghetto—found expression in this important Presidential speech: "We believe that our economic system should rest on a democratic foundation and that wealth should be created for the benefit of all. We have pledged our common resources to help one another in the hazards and struggles of individual life." The individual citizen, Truman declared, needed protection from the impersonal forces of an urban-industrial society, and the truly democratic society toward which he and his predecessor had been working must provide such protection. Now, Truman concluded, "Every segment of our population and every individual have a right to expect from our government a fair deal."[2]

The Fair Deal reform program that Truman presented to the Congress achieved only limited success. Perhaps the most important accomplishment of the Fair Deal was the preservation of New Deal reforms, not the creation of new programs. The opponents of the welfare state had been defeated in the election and could no longer hope for a wholesale repeal of the New Deal reforms; they retained great power within Congress, however, due in large part to the disproportionate rural representation in Congress. The cities might have determined the outcome of the Presidential election, but the rural areas still controlled Congress. The antireform element, comprised of right-wing Republicans and Southern Democrats, had its locus of power in the House of Representatives.[3] Although several secondary Fair Deal programs passed Congress,[4] this coalition prevented all but one of the major Fair Deal proposals from becoming law. Congress turned down an aid-to-education bill, a national health insurance program, a proposal to establish a Fair Employment Practices Commission, and the Brannan Plan and refused to repeal the Taft-Hartley Act. The one significant success—the housing bill that had been before Congress since 1945—passed a crucial test vote in the House by only five votes. The enactment of the national Housing Act of 1949, however, demonstrated the growing influence of urban liberalism in national politics and stands as a milestone in the broad sweep of twentieth-century reform.[5]

Housing and slum clearance, key reform objectives of urban liberalism, fitted perfectly within the basic framework of the Fair Deal. Slums and poor housing were beyond the power of individual cities or the private housing industry to solve. Despite the high rate of housing construction, the housing shortage, which had first arisen in the autumn of 1945, had not ended, but continued to mount, largely because of the high rate of marriages. Over 2½ million families still lived "doubled up," and over 5 million families lived in slum dwellings. Most significant was the fact that 30 per cent of all urban families had an annual income of less than $2,500, which meant that they could afford to pay no more than $27 a month for housing, including utilities. Slum and blighted sections covered 25 per cent of all urban areas in the nation and caused high losses in tax revenue for the cities and, conversely, caused a tremendous financial drain in police, health, and fire-protection costs.[6] Although the urban areas received most of the attention of Congress, the rural areas faced an equally serious housing problem. Twenty per cent of all farm dwellings needed major repairs; 67 per cent lacked running water; 80 per cent had no modern toilet facilities; and 40 per cent had no electricity.[7] Such statistics, shocking as they were to many congressmen, did not tell the entire story. Raymond M. Foley, Housing and Home Finance Administration chief, expressing the assumption of housing reform that good environment held the key to social uplift, told the Senate Banking and Currency Committee: "Figures and statistics show the extent of the deficit we have to meet. But they do not reflect the housing problem in terms of its threat to our way of life and our aspirations as a people and a democracy."[8]

Within a week after the election Truman released a statement affirming his intention to carry out his campaign pledges on housing. The election results, he said, were a "clear mandate" to enact the housing bill quickly. "The results," he said, "have strongly affirmed that the American people rank an effective housing program among the top domestic issues on which prompt action is demanded."[9] He reiterated this position in his Fair Deal message; the housing shortage, he told the Congress, remained serious and could best be met by immediate enactment of the comprehensive housing bill he had continually championed. Because the demand for low-cost housing was rapidly growing, he recommended that the number of public housing units be increased to at least one million.[10]

On the same day that Truman presented his Fair Deal message eight Democrats introduced the Administration's housing bill in the Senate. The bill called for 1,050,000 units of public housing to be constructed over a seven-year period, for $1 billion in loans and $500 million in capital grants to cities and states for slum clearance and urban redevelopment, for a program of housing research, and for $250 million in loans for repair of rural housing.[11] One hour before the eight Democrats introduced the bill Senator Allen J. Ellender notified Republican leader Robert A. Taft of the impending action and inquired if he wanted to add his name to the list of cosponsors. Because Taft did not have an opportunity to read the bill, he refused, and bipartisan sponsorship temporarily ended.[12] Even after he studied the bill Taft held a major reservation: the large number of public housing units to be built. Such a figure, he said, meant that about 25 per cent of all the housing would be federally subsidized, a situation that might easily provide "the opening wedge" to the nationalization of the housing industry. Taft also feared that this new bill would allow many families to live in public housing who could afford to pay for private housing. While he acknowledged that private enterprise had "failed to find a solution," Taft said he believed "very strongly that families able to pay their rent should not be subsidized."[13] He, therefore, decided to introduce an alternative housing bill, which Republicans Ralph Flanders and Irving Ives cosponsored with him. This bill differed from the Administration's bill only in the number of public housing units called for—600,000 units, to be built over a six-year period.[14]

Both sides quickly realized the need for bipartisan action if congressional approval of a workable housing bill was to be obtained. On January 9, Senator Ellender stated that the differences over the amount of public housing could easily be solved. Ives responded to his remark by pointing out that the Democrats had "slammed the door" on Taft after his continuous sponsorship for three years.[15] By January 27, when the three Republicans introduced their bill, Taft's anger over the snub had subsided; at this time he talked to reporters about the possibilities of resuming bipartisan support, which, he said, could readily be accomplished by the reduction of the number of public housing units.[16]

This *rapprochement* was achieved in the Senate Banking and Currency Committee. After listening to more than seventy-five witnesses over a three-week period, the committee reported a housing bill, sponsored by twenty senators, ten from each party, which provided for the construction of 810,000 units of public housing, to be built over a six-year period. The committee's report agreed with the basic premise of the Fair Deal philosophy: "It is unthinkable that this nation, the richest and most powerful in the world, will longer permit so many of its citizens to live and to grow up under the degrading and unhealthy conditions of the slums."[17] The comprehensive bill pleased both parties. "We wanted to get politics out of it," explained Committee Chairman Burnet Maybank (S.C.). "I hope the Senate will forget party politics and vote for public housing. If there ever was a bipartisan housing bill for the good of the poor people of this country, this is the bill."[18]

Before the Senate began debate on the comprehensive housing bill, it engaged in its annual fight over rent control. Because the housing shortage continued, Truman had called for a two-year extension of controls in his Fair Deal message. He requested that several control powers be strengthened to ensure a truly effective bill.[19] After the usual debate over the purpose of controls in a free enterprise system, Congress passed a bill including most of Truman's requests. The bill abolished the 15 per cent "voluntary" increase, stipulated heavy fines for evasion of controls, extended controls to trailers and residence hotels, and permitted the Housing Expediter to subpoena records of landlords. Most important, the Housing Expediter regained the power to control evictions, a power ended in 1947. The only request denied Truman was the extension of controls for two years; Congress cut the period to fifteen months.[20] This bill was much stronger than either of those passed by the Eightieth Congress. Truman readily signed it on March 30 and praised it for re-establishing "an effective system of rent control."[21]

On April 14 the Senate began consideration of the comprehensive housing bill. Debate lasted for seven days and centered around the freshman senator from Illinois, Paul H. Douglas. Formerly a professor of economics at the University of Chicago, Douglas emphasized the economic liability of slums and tenement housing. The nation's slums yielded only 6 per cent of the total urban revenue, he told the Senate, but absorbed 45 per cent of the service costs. To demonstrate the human aspect of the slum problem, Douglas displayed pictures of slums currently existing in Washington, D.C. Such areas, he declared, were "a moral cancer, a health hazard and an economic loss."[22] To dramatize the situation, Douglas guided four senators on a tour through two slum sections of the capital city, including "Schott's Alley," a dismal, refuse-littered area that stood within one hundred yards of the Senate Office Building.[23] What was observed on this much-publicized tour demonstrated the need for some program of slum clearance and low-cost housing and prompted the Republican *New York Herald-Tribune* to editorialize:

> The Senators' tour of the Washington slums says about all there is to say on the need for the long delayed na-

tional housing program. When Members of Congress may walk only 100 yards from their offices to find family after family crowded into unsanitary and condemned buildings because there is no place for them to live, the why of aid to housing is plain beyond argument.[24]

Two conservative Republicans, John Bricker (Ohio) and Harry Cain (Wash.), led the opposition. A desire to prevent further expansion of federal powers motivated the actions of both these men. Bricker held that the housing bill would only perpetuate "bureaucratic dictation" of local affairs, and Cain criticized the bill because it would result in "management, supervision and almost complete subsidy by the Federal Government."[25] These two foes of public housing argued, further, that housing problems should be handled locally: The individual cities should furnish a local solution to a local problem. Knowing that the support for the bill came, primarily, from two voting blocs, Southern senators and Northern liberals, they attempted to split this alliance by proposing an amendment that would forbid racial or ethnic discrimination in all public housing units built under the bill.[26] When several senators protested that such an amendment would kill the bill because the Southerners would then oppose it, Bricker exclaimed, "I have heard it said that this bill will not pass with this amendment. If it defeats the bill well and good. It will show there's something wrong with the bill itself or the platforms of both parties."[27]

Bricker's move prompted Senator Douglas to challenge the former vice-presidential candidate's motive. Although a staunch supporter of civil rights, Douglas urged Northern liberals, in this instance, to vote against the amendment because, if it passed, the votes of the Southern Democrats would defeat the entire housing bill. The amendment, Douglas acknowledged, "necessarily creates a sharp conflict within the hearts of all of us who want on one hand, to clear the slums and to provide decent housing for the slum dwellers and who, at the same time, feel very keenly that we should not treat any race as second-class citizens."[28] Douglas said that the Bricker-Cain amendment "would inevitably defeat the whole bill." Even if the Senate should adopt the amendment, Douglas charged, Bricker would not support the bill.[29] The freshman Senator concluded his speech, which lasted for well over one hour, by placing housing reform above civil rights. "I am ready to appeal to history and to time that it is in the best interests of the Negro race that we carry through the housing program as planned, rather than put in the bill an amendment which will inevitably defeat it, and defeat all hopes for rehousing 4,000,000 persons."[30] When the discrimination amendment came to a vote, most Northern liberals of both parties followed Douglas and joined with Southern Democrats to defeat the proposal by a vote of 49 to 31.[31] The next day, the Senate passed the housing bill by a 57-to-13 count.[32]

Even before the Senate began debate on the Administration's bill, Brent Spence, chairman of the House Banking and Currency Committee, introduced an identical bill in the House of Representatives.[33] The House committee began hearings on April 7, and on May 12, in a straight party vote, it approved the bill, 15 to 7.[34] The House Rules Committee, however, could not decide whether to grant the bill a rule and thus allow it to reach the House floor. Republican conservatives urged the committee to kill the bill. Minority Leader Joe Martin predicted that if the bill became law, total economic disaster would soon strike the nation:

> If you don't have the money you have got to do without them [slum clearance and public housing] for another year. I very seriously question whether we can embark on any new spending ventures when the Treasury is warning that there is going to be a deficit, with the possibility of higher taxes, which I believe will cause a crash and plunge us into a depression.[35]

Jesse Wolcott, Clarence Brown (Ohio), and Leo Allen also urged that the bill should not be sent to the House floor, arguing that it was "socialistic" and would cost the taxpayers dearly.[36] On June 7 the Rules Committee followed the advice of Martin and Wolcott by a 7-to-5 vote; three Southern Democrats voted with four Republican committee members to kill the bill.[37] Spence had anticipated such an occurrence and on the preceding day had introduced a resolution requesting the committee to report the bill. Under a new "antiblockade" rule, adopted in January, he could call the bill to the House floor twenty-one days later, thus bypassing the Rules Committee.[38] This did not occur, however, for the Rules Committee, under pressure from several sources, reversed its decision on June 14 and reported the bill by a vote of 8 to 4.[39]

With the bill on the House floor for the first time, after four years of effort, the real estate lobby intensified its opposition. *Headlines* urged every realtor to "be a Fanatic for Freedom" and to request his congressmen to oppose "the most dangerous piece of legislation of our generation." The newsletter also encouraged its readers to direct a large letter-telegram-telephone campaign toward their congressmen: "Tell [them] that all the organizations of 'fellow travelers' are for the bill as the most subtle means of breaking down American self-reliance and American self-rule."[40] Rodney Lockwood, president of the National Association of Home Builders, publicly criticized the bill as the product of "left wing pressure groups" and of those "who are looking to their socialized bureaucratic jobs."[41] T. H. Maenner, president of the National Association of Real Estate Boards, declared that the bill was "pure socialism" even though it did not nationalize all housing:

> Surely, if there is one thing clear about socialism, it is that it has never gained ascendance in one full blow. It always moves in bit by bit, eating away one area of free effort at a time until finally the people wake up and

find that everything is controlled at a central political headquarters. Then it is too late to make speeches about socialism.[42]

Incensed by such statements and by the pressures being exerted upon congressmen, Truman released a scathing criticism of the lobby and its methods:

> I do not recall ever having witnessed a more deliberate campaign of misrepresentation and distortion against legislation of such crucial importance to the public welfare. . . . These attempts to mislead and frighten the people and their representatives in the Congress—these false claims designed to prejudice some groups of the people against others—these malicious and willful appeals to ignorance and selfishness—are examples of selfish propaganda at its worst.[43]

On June 22, soon after the President's explosion, the House began consideration of the housing bill. The debate could not have begun more spectacularly; within a few minutes after the first speaker arose, a brief bout of fisticuffs erupted on the House floor. Eighty-three-year-old Adolph Sabath (Dem., Ill.), chairman of the Rules Committee, began the debate by criticizing the "unholy alliance and coalition" of Republicans and Southern Democrats that had prevented the bill from reaching the House floor for the preceding three years. Thereupon, fellow Democrat E. E. Cox, sixty-nine-year-old congressman from Georgia's rural Second District and a relentless opponent of the housing bill, reportedly called Sabath a liar and hit the Representative from Chicago in the mouth. Sabath's glasses fell to the floor, but he strenuously flailed away at his assailant and landed several blows before startled House members could stop the fracas.[44] Representative Cox, when he was finally recognized by the chair, criticized the bill as "a socialistic scheme" designed to create "a vast omnivorous bureaucracy" that would eventually eliminate all private housing in the United States.[45] The two

Democrats, whose action symbolized the urban-rural, liberal-conservative split within the Democratic party, soon forgave and forgot and posed for photographers in a partisan embrace.[46]

The debate, which was resumed in a more dignified manner, ended June 29. The most controversial amendment, which would strike out the public housing feature, failed by a vote of 209 to 204.[47] The housing bill then passed, 227 to 186.[48] Because the House bill called for the original number of public housing units—1,050,000—a conference with the Senate was required. The conferees accepted the Senate figure of 810,000 units, although three House members at the conference refused to sign the bill: Wolcott, Ralph Gamble, and Frederick C. Smith (Rep., Ohio). "The bill is just as bad as it was when it left the House," Wolcott informed reporters as he witnessed the passage of the bill that he had so ardently and resourcefully opposed for nearly four years.[49]

The supporters of the bill, however, believed it to be a major accomplishment. Taft called it "an historical occasion" and wrote Truman, "I am hopeful that the present Act will initiate a program of public and private housing which will lead to a solution of our housing difficulties, and bring about ultimately a condition in which decent housing is available to all."[50] Republican Charles Tobey was of the same mind,[51] as were the many interest groups that had supported the bill.[52]

The passage of the bill naturally pleased Truman. He wrote to Tobey, "I think we have done a good job on that piece of legislation and that we will never regret the passage of the bill."[53] On July 15, in the presence of several staunch supporters of the bill, Truman signed it into law,[54] thus culminating a movement that had begun early in the Second World War. The bill, Truman observed, adopted a national housing policy that declared it was the responsibility of the government to assure every American family of a decent home in a good environment. This, he believed, was "thor-

oughly consistent with American ideals and traditions." He
told reporters that he took

> deep satisfaction in the successful conclusion of the
> long fight for this legislation. I know this satisfaction is
> shared by the Members of Congress of both political
> parties and by the many private groups and individuals,
> who have supported this legislation over the past four
> years against ill-founded opposition.[55]

Truman achieved a rare legislative triumph with the passage of the Housing Act of 1949. Although the Democrats
dominated both houses of Congress by large majorities, the
bulk of Truman's Fair Deal never became law. For this reason
alone, the Housing Act is important within the matrix of
Fair Deal politics and stands as the most important single
Fair Deal measure passed by the Eighty-first Congress.[56]

Certainly, no one can completely explain the reasons behind any congressional vote, but certain tendencies do emerge
that help elucidate the defeat or success of a bill. The in-
clination of many congressmen to favor "liberal" or welfare
legislation added several names to the list in favor of the
comprehensive housing bill, as did the desire of many Democrats to support the Administration's bill. But the most important reason for the passage of the bill was the support it
received from congressmen who represented urban districts
or states.[57] A definite split between the rural-urban factions
was clearly evident in the House; a strong core of representatives from urban districts provided most of the support for
the bill in Congress, while a coalition of Southern Democrats and Republicans, coming primarily from rural districts,
comprised the opposition. Of the 193 Democrats who supported the bill, 144 represented urban districts, as did 25 of
the 33 Republicans who voted affirmatively. Ninety-four of
the 131 Republicans who opposed the bill represented rural
districts. Of the 55 Democrats who voted against the bill, 48
represented former Confederate states, and only 11 of the

negative Democratic votes were cast by urban representatives. The Southern Democratic-conservative Republican coalition in the House, therefore, posed a formidable obstacle to the housing program. The bill passed only because 47 Southern Democrats, who came predominantly from urban areas, supported the bill. However, in other areas, such as civil rights, these Southerners opposed Truman and provided the decisive margin of defeat.

Various reasons account for the refusal of the rural Southern Democrats to support the Administration. First, their districts would receive little benefit from the bill. More effective, however, was their fear of the expansion of federal powers at the expense of the states. They opposed, on principle, the idea of spending programs that weakened the powers of the individual states. Representative Cox cogently expressed this position: "I fear this new philosophy that threatens to sweep us away from the moorings of the Constitution. From a government of distributed powers, I have seen develop a virtual concentration of power. Rights reserved to the states are no longer respected."[58]

A strong conservative coalition was not present in the Senate. Few senators opposed the bill, largely because they realized that most states had serious housing and slum problems that must be solved. Unlike the representatives from the former Confederate states, the senators from the South strongly supported the bill. Only two Southern senators voted against the bill: Willis Robertson (Va.) and John McClellan (Ark.). A third Southerner, Harry Byrd of Virginia, did not vote, but announced his opposition to the bill. These three upheld the same conservative economic position as their counterparts in the lower chamber. Most Southern senators, however, viewed housing reform as did Allen J. Ellender. The southern states, with their rapidly growing urban areas, were encountering serious housing and slum problems, and the comprehensive housing bill offered an inexpensive and practical method of solving these problems. State and local powers, they believed, would be preserved by placing most of the responsibility for and control of public housing or urban redevelopment upon local officials; the federal government would provide only the money.

In addition to Taft, twenty-three Republican senators voted for the bill. While most of them came from states that had serious urban problems, some liberal Republicans, such as Ralph Flanders (Vt.) or Charles Tobey (N.H.), did not fall into this category. On the other hand, two Republicans— John Bricker of Ohio and William Knowland of California— opposed the bill even though they represented states with large urban areas; both followed their conservative political philosophies. The other nine negative Republican votes were cast by senators from such states as Montana, South Dakota, and Nebraska who followed closely the rural pattern.

The voting on the comprehensive bill, therefore, is best explained by a rural-urban split. This explanation, of course, is far from perfect, since many congressmen from rural areas supported the bill. But these were mostly Democrats who felt obligated to support the Administration or who generally voted the liberal line. Except for the rural Southerners in the House, the Democrats presented an almost solid front; their deviation was offset by a large number of Republicans who represented urban districts and states or who believed the bill to be vital to the nation's welfare.

The Housing Act of 1949 gave Truman a rare moment of legislative success on a major domestic reform program and, by establishing large-scale programs of public housing and urban redevelopment, was a turning point in the history of housing reform. The act also made another important contribution to the housing reform movement: It contained a national housing policy that stated the federal government's responsibility to insure to every American family "a decent home and a suitable living environment."[59] Truman clearly realized the implications of this policy and wholeheartedly endorsed it:

> Here, for the first time in our history, is a declaration by the people of the United States, through their Congress, that every American, regardless of his income or origin, is entitled to an opportunity to obtain decent housing. It is one of the most significant actions taken by the Congress in recent years.[60]

Thus, in the area of housing and urban redevelopment, the Fair Deal was successful, although by only a razor-thin margin.

Chapter IX

The Final Years

F ROM THE TIME of the passage of the Housing Act of 1949 until Harry S Truman left office, four diverse aspects of housing policy occupied his Administration's attention. In 1950 the Administration attempted to extend assistance to middle-income families by proposing an elaborate program designed to aid the construction of privately owned housing cooperatives. At the same time, the gradual elimination of rent controls had to be accomplished without causing undue injury to either tenants or landlords. The postwar drive for first-class citizenship for the American Negro forced the Administration to develop a policy with regard to discrimination in federal-financed housing. Finally and most important, the high goals of the Housing Act of 1949 had to be translated into cleared slums and public housing developments.

Two unrelated factors prevented the accomplishment of these goals, however. The successful passage of the comprehensive housing bill, instead of stimulating housing reformers to carry out the programs immediately, had just the opposite effect. By mid-century, enthusiasm for housing reform had

116

dissipated. Many liberals, in response to the activities of Senator Joseph R. McCarthy, turned their attention to civil liberties and left housing reform to the professional "housers" and the Truman Administration.[1] The sudden eruption of war in Korea in mid-1950 had equal impact because it forced the Administration to refocus its housing policies in relationship to military requirements. The war, of course, curtailed or severely limited expensive domestic programs.

The decline in enthusiasm for housing reform resulted primarily from the high rate of housing construction during the postwar years. Because the housing reformers were few in numbers and poorly organized, the reform movement had derived its power from the widespread popular discontent created by the housing shortage. A handful of housing reformers had taken advantage of the situation and transformed public opinion into a strong movement, which culminated in securing the passage of the Housing Act of 1949. By 1950, however, several years of peak construction had ended the shortage and, thereby, mollified public opinion. During the years 1946-1949, approximately 3,476,200 housing units had been built, and this was topped by the all-time high of 1,396,000 in 1950.[2] This record rate of construction appeased the cries of the public for housing reform and sapped the effectiveness of the housing reformers. This, in turn, left the Administration without an effective ally for its housing program during the last three years of Truman's Presidency.

The loss of public support for housing reform became clearly evident in the early months of 1950 when the Administration attempted to extend governmental assistance to the so-called "middle-income" families. The Housing Act of 1949 set forth as national policy the goal of a decent house for every American family, but it did not include a program by which to attain this end. The New Deal had devised the mortgage insurance program of the Federal Housing Administration, which supposedly helped families with incomes in the uppermost third to purchase houses.[3] Public housing, begun in

1937 and greatly expanded in 1949, had theoretically provided families in the lowest third with the means to obtain decent housing. Sandwiched in between these two groups was the "forgotten one-third," the families that had incomes approximately between $2,700 and $4,300. Truman believed this group deserved the opportunity to acquire better housing than they could afford by conventional means.[4]

High costs, created by a lag in housing technology and by the disorganization of the housing industry, prevented the "forgotten one-third" from enjoying better housing. To solve this problem, the Truman Administration proposed the establishment of privately owned housing cooperatives, which could receive 50-year, low-interest loans from the government-sponsored National Mortgage Company. Cooperative borrowing and construction would cut costs, the Administration argued, and enable participating middle-income families to enjoy better housing at lower costs. The Administration pointed to the Rural Electrification Administration as an example of a successful cooperative enterprise. The bill also included provisions for loans to colleges for student housing and for FHA loans to builders of large apartment buildings.[5]

The drive for cooperative housing began in June, 1949, when Senator John Sparkman of Alabama introduced a bill intended to initiate such housing.[6] The Truman Administration, preoccupied with the legislative struggle leading to the Housing Act of 1949, paid little attention to the plan, and it died in committee. In late 1949, however, housing reformers took active interest in the bill and began a campaign to win congressional approval for it.[7] The cooperative idea appealed to Truman because it provided a workable method of helping a group of citizens he considered to be "the backbone of this country."[8] In his State of the Union message in 1950 he gave the program his wholehearted support.[9]

Although the bill provided a way for a large segment of the population to join together to provide themselves with good housing at low costs, the real estate lobby opposed the program. The lobby, still under the leadership of Herbert U. Nelson, disliked the bill for the same reason that it had disliked public housing: It would extend governmental housing activity. The industry argued that no need existed for such a program and cited the high postwar construction rates to support its position. Because the program was unnecessary, the lobby contended, it would increase inflationary pressures.[10] Even though the cooperative plan would foster the construction of privately owned housing developments, the lobby branded the program as "pure socialism."[11] The United States Savings and Loan League, quite understandably, was the most severe critic of the plan. This organization based its opposition upon the low interest rate to be charged by the proposed government lending agency. The suggested rate of 3¼ per cent, the league charged, created unfair competition for private lending companies. The league obviously feared a considerable loss of business for its member institutions.[12]

After a stormy hearing, the cooperative bill reached the Senate floor on March 14, 1950, but in altered form. The committee had eliminated the proposal to create a separate lending corporation by placing the responsibility directly under the Housing and Home Finance Agency. It had also slashed the amount of money available for loans in one year from $2,000,000 to $1,250,000.[13]

Unlike the comprehensive housing bill, the cooperative plan received little public support. Even many Democrats had serious reservations about the plan. Because no ground swell of public enthusiasm developed, the bill's sponsors never convinced dubious congressmen that a need existed which merited such a large outlay of federal funds.[14] Senators John Bricker and Harry Cain, not suprisingly, led the opposition in debate. Although the bill, which would enable about 250,000 families to own their own homes, appeared to many to be a private housing bill designed to prevent nationalization of housing, Bricker believed that the plan was another step toward socialism. He voiced fear of the possible consequences of Americans "living in a group society" instead of in a traditional one-family home.[15] The basic argument used in debate against the bill rested on the low interest rate on cooperative loans, which, opponents said, discriminated against veterans, who paid at least 1 per cent higher under other government programs. This argument ignored the facts that all veterans' groups supported the bill and that a large number of veterans would participate in the cooperative program.[16]

The decisive action with regard to the bill was the vote taken on an amendment, proposed by Bricker, that would strip from the bill its provision for loans to housing cooperatives. A significant number of Democrats deserted the Administration, which enabled passage of the amendment; thirteen Democrats, ten of them from the South, voted with thirty Republicans to kill the program for loans by a count of 43 to 38.[17] Several of the Democrats who opposed the cooperative bill had supported the Housing Act of 1949.[18] Their opposition was due to aversion to the creation of another federal program, especially since it did not seem to be so desperately needed as the program for public housing and slum clearance. The fear of the inflationary pressures that might result was another major point of agreement between the Republicans and Southern Democrats. No large quantities of public-opinion mail descended upon Washington as they had in 1949.[19] To be sure, the long list of lobby groups lined up behind the bill as in the past, but their efforts lacked the important support of an aroused public. The plight of the "forgotten one-third" was quite undramatic when compared to the situation of the dwellers in Schott's Alley.

After the Senate stripped the cooperative program from the housing bill, the Administration hoped to salvage the program in the House of Representatives. Truman urged the House to pass the plan, which, he said, would meet a "large unfilled need."[20] His effort failed; the House duplicated the Senate's action by a vote of 218 to 155.[21] Eighty-one Democrats, mostly Southerners, supported Jesse Wolcott's motion to strike the cooperative feature from the bill. With the controversial part of the bill removed, the House speedily passed the remainder of the bill on April 6.[22] A conference with the Senate adjusted cost differences in the minor programs that remained, and Truman signed the bill on April 20.[23] Unlike his practice in previous years when Congress had refused to pass his housing program, he did not release a statement criticizing the Congress. The fact that a significant portion of his own party had not supported the bill probably caused Truman's silence.

Although the Democratic Eighty-first Congress failed to pass the Administration's middle-income cooperative program, it did approve Truman's request to extend rent controls. In his State of the Union message of 1950, Truman pointed out that, although the postwar shortage no longer could be termed critical, a complete end to controls would cause serious financial problems for several million tenants.[24] Actually, the number of units still under control had been cut in half since the end of the Second World War by the actions of local decontrol boards; approximately 8,000,000 units remained under controls in January of 1950. The failure of many cities and states to enact their own control laws had prompted Truman to request one final year of controls. "Despite the record volume of housing production in recent years," he told Congress, "only in the past two years have we begun to catch-up on the accumulated shortage." Truman feared that an abrupt end of controls would "precipitate a wave of exorbitant rent increase," which would do serious injury to the citizens who could least afford to pay higher rents.[25] His efforts to continue controls met stiff opposition from the landlords, who claimed that the high rate of postwar housing construction had ended the shortage.[26] The problems surrounding rent controls resulted from the fact that many cities had solved their housing shortage, while others had not. Clearly, from an over-all view, the housing supply justified another twelve-month extension of controls. Many congressmen, however, had grown dissatisfied with the entire program. Their unwillingness to support controls reflected the local political pressures that the landlords, working through the real estate lobby, were exerting against them. Many Democrats who previously had voted for controls told Majority Leader John McCormack that they "could not go along any more."[27] The Administration had to exert its full influence to get the bill passed and then had to compromise by reducing the extension period to six months.

As usual, Congress waited until the last month to debate the proposed control bill. With controls scheduled to end on June 30, the Senate took the bill under consideration on June 7. A twelve-hour filibuster by Harry Cain highlighted the ensuing debate. He charged, among other things, that controls were an illegal invasion of private property that led landlords into "involuntary servitude."[28] Cain agreed to end his filibuster if a vote on a motion to return the bill to committee were called. This motion failed by 44 to 25; the bill then passed the Senate, 36 to 28.[29] After a limited debate the House passed a similar bill on June 13, 202 to 163,[30] and a conference on June 23 ironed out minor differences. Truman signed the bill without comment, although Housing Expediter Tighe Woods urged Truman to accompany the signing with the announcement that this would be final extension of rent controls. Woods wanted to warn state and city governments to enact their own control bills before federal controls elapsed. The reluctance of many Democrats to support the present extension, Woods pointed out, indicated that any future extension would be very difficult to obtain;[31] party loyalty could go only so far.

Woods's memorandum reached the White House just five days before the fateful day of June 25, 1950—the beginning of the Korean War. After the start of the conflict, rent controls reverted temporarily to a wartime basis. They were now needed to help prevent inflation and to protect tenants who moved into new areas to work in defense factories. Controls did not end on January 1, 1951, as Truman had planned, but were extended for ninety days at the urging of Stuart Symington, chairman of the National Securities Resources Board.[32] The purpose of this stop-gap measure, passed during the lameduck session of the Eighty-first Congress, was to continue controls until the new Congress could study the problem from a fresh perspective. The new Congress decided that the war effort, for the most part, did not require a nationwide blanket of rent controls and passed a final ninety-day control law to give individual cities an opportunity to pass local controls if they were needed.[33] Rent controls finally ended on June 30, 1951, although under the provisions of the Defense Act of 1951, Congress could maintain controls in critical defense areas, if necessary, until the Korean conflict ended.[34]

While the Truman Administration wrestled with its middle-income housing program and rent controls, it also had to concern itself with another problem, which was completely unrelated to either of the others. When Senators Bricker and Cain introduced their amendment against discrimination during the debate on the comprehensive housing bill in 1949, they brought to national attention the issue of housing segregation. Truman had demonstrated his interest in the welfare of the Negro when he established the Committee on Civil Rights.[35] Although the committee, when it issued its report, did not deal with housing in detail, it did point out clearly the problem of segregation in this area. The Bricker-Cain amendment came approximately thirty years after the beginning of the great migration of the Negroes from southern farms to northern cities. This northern-urbanward migration soon led to a concerted postwar effort to attain full civil rights for Negro Americans. The Administration was now faced with the need to devise a policy on housing segregation that would please the Negroes, the Northern liberals, and the Southern segregationists in the Democratic party. Although

Housing Administrator Raymond M. Foley did not sympathize with segregation, he did realize that many southern cities needed public housing. If the Administration adopted a firm nonsegregation policy for public housing projects, the end of public housing in the South would result. It would also mean increased opposition in the South to future appropriation bills for public housing. Confronted by this delicate situation, Foley adopted the policy of allowing the local housing authorities to determine whether discrimination should be practiced in their local programs.[36] Actually, 38 per cent of all public housing units were occupied by Negroes, even though in all southern cities and in many northern ones the races were carefully separated.[37] The "separate but equal" doctrine, although in its twilight stage, was still the law of the land, and Foley embraced it as the best way to appease all sides and still maintain the public housing program. This policy apparently solved the problem created by the Bricker-Cain amendment to the satisfaction of most interested groups, for no serious repercussions resulted from Foley's policy until the Eisenhower era.

The spokesmen for the Negroes were far more interested in the policy followed by the Federal Housing Administration than that followed by the Public Housing Administration. Since its inception, FHA had followed a conservative business philosophy. Because housing for Negroes was considered a poor investment risk, FHA had consistently refused to underwrite housing in areas threatened by "Negro invasion." The FHA likewise refused to insure loans on most housing for Negroes. Its underwriting manuals explicitly warned of the infiltration of "unharmonious racial groups" and pointed out that neighborhood stability was vital to maintaining property values and depended upon occupancy by "the same social and racial classes." In 1947 the manual said, "Protective covenants are essential to the sound development of proposed residential areas since they regulate the use of the land and provide a basis for the development of harmonious, attractive neighborhoods."[38] The National Association for the Advancement of Colored People did not exaggerate when it charged that FHA helped create and maintain "black ghettos."[39] In early 1950 Foley announced that FHA would no longer insure a mortgage if the contract contained a written "restrictive covenant." This belated announcement came two years after the Supreme Court had ruled that restrictive covenants, although not unconstitutional, were not legally enforceable.[40] As realtors soon learned, however, the new policy on mortgages applied only to the construction of new houses, and FHA underwriters did not protest if unwritten "gentlemen's agreements" were reached. Thus, while the new FHA policy drew praise from Negro groups, it had little immediate effect upon the traditional discrimination policy.[41]

Although the three problems discussed above were directly related to the Administration's housing program and its success, the most important concern of the Administration was the implementation of the Housing Act of 1949. The formidable task of converting the high goals of the act into actual houses and cleared slums was beset with many difficulties. It is not surprising, therefore, that by the expiration of the Administration's term of office, forty-three months after the comprehensive bill became law, fewer than 60,000 of the authorized 810,000 units of public housing had been constructed and only twenty-six slum clearance projects had been started.[42]

The complex process that a community had to follow provided one major reason for this slow start. In order to qualify for public housing, the community had to: (1) establish a local housing authority under state law; (2) prepare a detailed project proposal and obtain approval from the local governing body; (3) procure from the local government an agreement to furnish 10 per cent of the entire cost of the project; (4) demonstrate to the Public Housing Administration that a need existed; and (5) get PHA's approval of the detailed construction plans for the project. The procedure for receiving funds for slum clearance and urban redevelopment was similar, except for the added requirement that the redevelopment project had to conform to the city's master plan.[43]

This elaborate machinery, a delicate balance of federal and local powers, obviously was not conducive to quick action. The initiation and management of a public housing project required that interested citizens in the community devote time and effort to the local project. Each community, of course, had its own particular problems, but a difficulty that plagued most authorities was lack of public support. Slum housing actually concerned few citizens directly, and if individuals did become interested, the elaborate procedure seemed, in many instances, too difficult and complex to undertake. Public indifference, therefore, frustrated the efforts of the local housing authority in many cities.[44] Also, the local authorities seldom had professional assistance to guide them in their endeavors, and, consequently, they frequently made technical errors that caused long delays. One of the most common of these errors was to submit plans to the PHA that did not conform to the regulation concerning the maximum cost per room, established by the 1949 law. In 1950 and 1951 the PHA had to reject proposals for over 6,000 units because their cost exceeded the $1,750 per-room limit. Some of the proposals that were rejected, according to Public Housing Commissioner John T. Egan, were almost luxurious.[45] If a plan was not approved, the local authority had to draft new plans.

Many communities, however, never reached the stage of submitting plans to the Public Housing Administration because the real estate lobby succeeded in its efforts to block public housing at the local level. Since the responsibility for initiating a project rested with the local community, the lobby decided to move its operations to that level. Immediately after the passage of the Housing Act of 1949, the lobby devised plans to thwart public housing in each community where it would be proposed. The National Association of Home Builders, in collaboration with its companion trade associations, sent "public education kits" to local leaders who wanted to fight public housing. These kits contained explicit instructions on how to successfully oppose the local housing authority.[46]

The lobby, basing its local campaigns upon the assumption that the general public was uninformed, ignorant, and selfish, played upon local prejudices and distorted facts without hesitation. It also shrewdly exploited racial prejudices and fears of federal domination. The same "canned" editorials and advertisements appeared in urban areas throughout the nation. The following lead advertisements, for example, appeared in many cities: "There are too many Jokers in the Public Housing Deal"; "Can You Afford to Pay Somebody Else's Rent?"; "Government Operated Politically Controlled Housing has no Place in the American Plan of Living"; and "Public Housing means the End of Racial Segregation in Savannah!" Other methods, varying with the community, were also used. In Oakland, California, for example, sound trucks toured the city the day before a crucial vote in the council, announcing, "Your homes will be torn down! The Oakland City Council is voting on a socialized housing project." In many instances, when the time neared for the voting on an important housing issue, national leaders arrived to direct the opposition. And, of course, realtors, lenders, and contractors privately used their positions within the community to put pressure upon the newspapers for editorials or upon council members for votes against public housing proposals.[47] If the lobby was not successful in its efforts to keep the local governments from adopting plans for public housing and sending them to Washington for PHA's approval, it then sought to force a public referendum upon the proposed project, which would enable the lobby to wage a full-scale propaganda campaign. By the end of 1951 thirty-eight such referendums had been held, and in twenty-five cases the real estate lobby emerged victorious.[48]

In the face of this determined and resourceful opposition the housing reformers were unable to mount an effective counter-offensive. The four-year struggle to get the comprehensive bill through Congress had exhausted the impulse behind the reform movement. Whereas the real estate lobby possessed vigorous, able leadership and received enthusiastic support from a militant organization that reached into every community in the nation, the housing reformers were disorganized and lacked effective guidance. The National Public Housing Conference, the only national organization that had as its primary purpose the establishment of public housing, claimed only four thousand members, and most of these were professional housing officials and welfare workers. The conference also lacked the financial resources and local roots that helped the real estate lobby to be so effective. While altruism motivated the NPHC, important financial and psychological motives influenced the actions of the real estate lobby.[49]

Housing reform, therefore, was rudderless; inexperienced local officials were no match for the well-organized and well-trained opposition. Even the National Public Housing Conference was impotent. Executive Vice-President Lee Johnson, a former PHA employee, was virtually unknown outside of the housing reform movement, and the lack of an effective grass-roots organization and of sufficient finances prevented him from becoming better known. Housing reform desperately needed a prominent national figure to revive national interest, but none was forthcoming. President Truman obviously was deeply interested in housing reform, but he could devote only a limited amount of his time to the matter, especially after the Korean conflict began. Poor health had forced the retirement of the one man who could have provided the necessary leadership—Senator Robert F. Wagner. His departure from politics left a vacuum in the movement, and no person of his abilities or stature emerged to take his place. Consequently, within a year after the passage of the Housing Act of 1949, the entire housing reform movement had become stagnant.[50]

With the real estate lobby now placing housing reform on the defensive for the first time since 1933, reform leadership necessarily fell by default to the Truman Administration; even Lee Johnson appealed to the Administration for help.[51] But Truman's housing director, Raymond M. Foley, did not possess the leadership qualities necessary to turn the promises of the Housing Act of 1949 into reality. Foley, a quiet, uninspiring man, possessed only a limited imagination and had continually spurned previous opportunities to lead housing reform. He looked upon his position as solely administrative and declined to propose new ideas or even to make major decisions without White House approval. Although Foley was an able administrator and his bureaucracy was recognized as one of the most efficient agencies in Washington, he never forged new patterns for action.[52] On many occasions Foley's hesitancy reflected his own indecisiveness on public housing. He never seemed to have resolved his own position on this issue, for he continually strove to please both the reformers and the real estate lobby.[53] To be sure, he did support public housing, but he invariably prefaced any endorsement of it with an affirmation of his unquestioning faith in the private housing industry.[54] His support for public housing lacked enthusiasm and usually seemed apologetic. To the end he remained a "safe FHA man" who continually boosted private housing, and, in return, he received accolades for his "fairness" from the leadership of the real estate lobby.[55]

Instead of actively assisting the local communities with the formulation of their plans, the Washington offices of the PHA and the HHFA allowed the inexperienced authorities to make many time-consuming mistakes; and, instead of boldly attacking the opponents to his agency's program, Foley gave the real estate lobby a free hand in its local obstructionistic activities. He was already on public record as saying that he could understand the lobby's reasons for conducting such opposition.[56] His general attitude is reflected in the fact that the PHA did not even have ready the forms necessary for the local authorities to make application for public housing funds until December of 1949.[57] Even Lee Johnson, a consistent friend of the Administration's housing policies, grew critical of the HHFA by late 1950 when he saw the effects of the nonchalant administration of the public housing program. "In our opinion," he wrote privately to Truman, "timidity, inability to make critical decisions, and a lack of constructive, dynamic leadership have been the principal contributing factors to little progress in the public low-rent housing field."[58] Presidential aides Richard Neustadt and David D. Lloyd conducted a private investigation and confirmed Johnson's judgment. They reported that the record of the eighteen months following the passage of the act was, at best, "mighty modest" and that the major cause lay in the leadership of the HHFA.[59] Thus, the combination of general lethargy in the housing movement, a militant real estate lobby, and a stodgy housing administration largely circumscribed the public housing program.

The real estate lobby also received considerable help for its cause from an unexpected source; the outbreak of the Korean War applied the *coup de grâce* to the high hopes of urban liberals for a break-through in housing reform. Within three weeks after the North Korean troops crossed the 38th parallel, President Truman began to place the nation on a wartime footing. On July 18, by executive order, he limited the number of public housing units to be constructed during the last six months of 1950 to 30,000, simultaneously reduced by 50 per cent the amount of insurance the Federal Housing Administration could authorize, and raised by 5 per cent the down payment for all its loans.[60] Truman hoped that these measures would conserve materials and reduce inflationary pressures, but he also realized that his actions meant that the goals of the Housing Act of 1949 would not be reached. Housing reformers, seeing their program virtually curtailed, vigorously opposed these drastic moves; they foresaw the possible scuttling of the entire public housing program. "We regret that the only action so far taken has seriously restricted the vitally needed public housing program, while only superficial measures have been applied to the private housing field," they protested.[61]

The destructive measures that the reformers feared were soon forthcoming. On October 17, 1950, the Federal Reserve Board, in conjunction with Foley, promulgated Regulation X, which imposed, under the Defense Production Act, further curbs upon housing construction.[62] The heart of Regulation X was a graduated scale of down-payment requirements for a FHA loan; it called for a down payment of 10 per cent on a home costing less than $5,000 and a steady increase, in stages, to 50 per cent on homes selling for over $25,000. According to housing reformers, real estate agents, and lenders, who curiously found themselves in agreement, this rigid anti-inflation decree would practically eliminate home buying among the lower- and middle-income families.[63] This prediction proved correct, as housing construction declined by more than 25 per cent in 1951 from the peak year of 1950.[64]

What remained of the public housing program also received a new orientation. Following the outbreak of hostilities, the Public Housing Administration judged proposed projects according to their possible contributions to the war effort. Decent housing for slum dwellers was postponed until after the war.[65] Because the slum clearance program required a long period of original planning, this phase of the Housing Act of 1949 posed no threat of inflation and therefore did not receive any limitations. By the time Truman left office it had scarcely reached the construction stage.[66]

Although Truman restricted public housing in his war effort, he had no intention of allowing it to be completely eliminated. At the end of 1950 he decided that public housing could provide much of the needed defense housing. Fearing that his early restrictions would lead to the eventual elimination of public housing altogether, he set no restriction upon public housing construction for the first six months of 1951. During this period PHA approved 59,703 units.[67]

The opponents of public housing realized that the Korean conflict offered a good opportunity to kill the entire program. In 1951 two congressmen from Texas, Edward Gossett and Albert Thomas, attempted to restrict the total number of public housing units to be constructed for the next fiscal year to just 5,000.[68] Such action would indeed have killed the entire public housing program. Truman had urged Congress to authorize 75,000 units for the year, most of which would be used to provide housing for defense workers. He vigorously opposed the attempt to eliminate public housing by cutting the appropriations and wrote to Senator Burnet Maybank: "To all intents and purposes this means repealing the public housing provision of the Housing Act of 1949. That was one of the best laws to be passed by a recent Congress. We need it now as much as ever." The proposed restriction, he continued, "would cripple the program for national defense in many parts of the country and thereby impede and imperil the national security."[69] Congress agreed with Truman and defeated the Gossett-Thomas proposal, although it did reduce Truman's request for 75,000 units by a third. Congress then approved the same figure of 50,000 for the next fiscal year.[70]

The final years of Truman's Presidency were spent under the cloud of the Korean conflict. This conflict forced a reassessment of many domestic programs, including the housing programs. A decline in the spirit of housing reform and a nonchalant housing administration, however, contributed directly to the failure of the public housing program to achieve its potential and was partially responsible for the defeat in Congress of the housing bill for middle-income families.

Chapter X

Conclusion

SINCE LEAVING the White House, Harry S Truman has frequently remarked that his place in history cannot be accurately assessed until fifty years have elapsed. In regard to foreign policy this is true, since several of the policies he inaugurated have not reached their final development and because most documents related to this critical area are not yet available to researchers. But in the field of domestic policy the historian can now, justifiably, advance interpretations based upon rich manuscript collections and the seemingly endless stream of published materials.

As this study has indicated, the Truman housing program, because it was too deeply involved in the complexities of national affairs, cannot be isolated from other developments. Truman had no clear-cut policy on housing when he assumed the Presidency, but early in his Administration he enthusiastically assumed leadership for a comprehensive reform program that had been formulated during the war years. Truman's belief that the government should be the instrument of social improvement meshed neatly with the assumptions of social regeneration that the housing reform movement advocated, which could be traced back through the New Deal to the progressive era.

Unlike his predecessors, Truman believed in government's social role to the degree that he threw the full weight of the Presidency behind housing reform. He strongly believed that slums and poor housing were inexcusable in a nation as powerful and affluent as the United States and fully realized the embarrassing incongruity in the fact that, although his nation possessed an abundance of wealth and was one of the greatest powers of the world, millions of Americans lived in squalid tenements. America could harness atomic energy, conquer Germany and Japan, and almost overnight rebuild Western Europe, but it could not arrest the growth of slums or eradicate poor housing in its own cities.

Housing reform stands as a lonely monument to the basic legislative objectives of the Fair Deal. As did other urban-oriented reforms, housing ran afoul the tenacious antireform coalition in Congress that had roots reaching deeply into rural America. Only by the narrowest of margins did the Housing Act of 1949 pass Congress; on a test vote in the House of Representatives it escaped the clutches of the conservative coalition by just five votes. Housing legislation succeeded where other Fair Deal measures failed only because it had the overwhelming support of the public. The public pressure, however, resulted from the tremendous postwar housing shortage and was only indirectly related to the problems of low-income housing and slum clearance. Had the opposition succeeded in blocking passage in 1949, the "comprehensive" legislation probably would never have become law, because public enthusiasm for reform dwindled as the housing shortage rapidly disappeared.

Housing also played a significant role in the tumultuous political arena of the Truman era. Both the annual struggle over rent controls and the far-reaching political implications of the abortive Veterans' Emergency Housing Program document the explosive nature of this issue. A veteran unable to locate a house or apartment for his family posed far more than just a humanitarian problem; he confronted Truman with a political crisis. The congressional campaigns of 1946, in which Republicans asked, "Had Enough?" and the 1948 campaign in which Truman emphasized housing legislation to his urban audiences illustrate the political significance of housing.

The frequent inner contradictions of Truman's housing policies reflect the complexity of the problems that confronted the Missourian. Torn between such advisers as Wilson Wyatt, who continually urged more governmental action, and John W. Snyder, who pressed equally hard for less, or between the demands of urban liberals and those of the politically potent real estate lobby, Truman gave every appearance of staunch liberalism in his housing policies, but in the day-to-day conduct of his housing agency he closely adhered to the real estate lobby's position. While Truman echoed the demands of militant housing reformers for expansive programs of slum clearance and public housing, his administrator Raymond M. Foley continually assured the housing industry that all would be well. Significantly, the Truman Administration met all of the demands of the housing industry by enacting such programs as yield insurance and expansion of the activities of the Federal Housing Administration; it differed with the industry only on the matter of public housing.

Thus, Truman's housing policies, in retrospect, seem to support Samuel Lubell's interpretation that Truman was a man who "bought time."[1] Caught in the political vise formed by the forces of conservatism and reform, Truman frequently talked to satisfy one group and acted to please the other. The failure to convert the lofty goals of the Housing Act of 1949 into the actuality of houses and cleared slums illustrates that Truman operated in a period of political stalemate. In a national election his liberalism carried the day, but in Congress, where these objectives had to be enacted and the necessary funds appropriated, the rural coalition exerted its full power.

Hailed as a major achievement by housing reformers, the Housing Act of 1949 has proven to be a hollow victory. For an accurate analysis, the act must be judged primarily on the basis of the performance of the central part of the legislation—public housing. The widespread disaffection with public housing is perhaps best demonstrated by the lack of opposition now offered by the formerly active real estate lobby. By 1960 many of the most vocal supporters of public housing during the Truman Administration had become openly critical of the program. The real estate lobby felt that organized opposition was no longer necessary.[2] Even to its most enthusiastic supporters, public housing has been a great disappointment; to its critics, its failures have only confirmed their earlier predictions; to the social scientists, the inadequacies of public housing have further documented the growing belief that social regeneration cannot be achieved within a span of a few years or even within a generation.[3] Indeed, in this day when neo-orthodoxy is gaining wide acceptance and political conservatism is seemingly on the upswing, the failures of public housing add weighty evidence to the argument that, although the reconstruction of slums is possible, the expected simultaneous reconstruction of human nature is nearly impossible.

The Housing Act of 1949 called for the erection of 810,000 units of public housing over a six-year period. By July 1, 1964, more than fifteen years after the passage of the now oft-amended law, only 356,203 units had been built.[4] More families lived in substandard housing in 1965 than in 1949. The inexorable spread of slums in the "inner core" of the nation's cities now threatens to spread to the suburbs constructed during the postwar period, including many jerry-built housing tracts erected under the Veterans' Emergency Housing Program. While the legislation has been inadequate to provide standard housing to meet even the needs in 1949, the continued growth of the urban population has intensified the seemingly perpetual problem of slum housing.[5]

The limited scope of the original legislation helps explain the shortcomings of the program. The authorized 810,000 units were only a fraction of the need in 1949, and Congress continually refused even to appropriate sufficient funds to construct the authorized number of dwellings. During the Korean conflict the Truman Administration drastically reduced the annual maximum number of units to 50,000, and in 1954 the Eisenhower Administration set as the maximum construction figure 35,000 units a year.

The major source of disillusionment, however, has been the failure of public housing to fulfill the high aspirations of the housing reformers—to reduce the social disorders of crime, vice, broken families, and juvenile delinquency. This failure is succinctly summarized in the lament of a former public housing official:

> Once upon a time we thought that if we could only get our problem families out of those dreadful slums, then papa would stop taking dope, mama would stop chasing around, and Junior would stop carrying a knife. Well, we've got them in a nice new apartment with modern kitchens and a recreation center. And they're still the same bunch of bastards they always were.[6]

Even uncleanliness and dilapidation have not been appreciably reduced. As Jane Jacobs, Harrison Salisbury, various housing experts, and several social scientists have clearly demonstrated, public housing has only perpetuated the exact problems it sought to eradicate.[7] In her perceptive criticism of slum clearance and public housing, Jane Jacobs concludes that public housing projects "have become worse centers of delinquency, vandalism and general social hopelessness than the slums they were supposed to replace."[8] "In too many instances," Salisbury says, "we have merely institutionalized

our slums."[9] In his vivid, firsthand description of the Fort
Greene project in New York City, he describes conditions that
are common to many projects throughout the nation:

> The same shoddy shiftlessness, the broken windows,
> the missing light bulbs, the plaster cracking from the
> walls, the pilfered hardware, the cold, drafty corridors,
> the doors on sagging hinges, the acid smell of sweat and
> cabbage, the ragged children, the playgrounds that are
> seas of muddy clay, the bruised and battered trees, the
> ragged clumps of grass, the planned absence of art,
> beauty or taste, the gigantic masses of brick, of con-
> crete, of asphalt, the inhuman genius with which our
> know-how has been perverted to create human cesspools
> worse than those of yesterday.[10]

Although many exceptions to this description do exist, the
general widespread criticism of public housing throughout
the nation suggests that public housing, as now established,
too often conforms to the Fort Greene pattern.

The failure of public housing to remake the character of
the inhabitants into constructive citizens, as originally argued,
has led to the inevitable conclusion that poor housing does
not lie at the root of the other problems of social disorder,
but is another manifestation of the same problems. Poor
housing now seems to be merely another condition caused
by the entire environment generally associated with poverty,
low cultural aspirations, poor education, and unhealthy basic
attitudes toward personal and family conduct. Thus, the
specters of public housing elevators serving as convenient
toilets, of staircases becoming places for muggings, of the
project area becoming a breeding ground for teen-age gang
activities, and of the general, all-too-familiar unkempt appearance of public housing projects rise from the same psychological and cultural factors that produce tenement areas.
In short, because poor housing results from and is not the
basic cause of other social and cultural malconditions, public
housing has proved incapable of achieving the high goals

set for it by its promoters during the Truman period. The real failure, therefore, does not lie in its inability to elevate the conduct of its inhabitants, but rather in the original assumption that poor housing lies at the root of most other urban social disorders.[11]

Many explanations are advanced for what housing reform leader Catharine Bauer has called "the dreary deadlock of public housing."[12] Obviously, one major cause of difficulty is the administrative structure. Confined in a bureaucratic strait jacket, local housing authority officials are forced to conform to minutely described procedures. Indirectly, the opponents of public housing have increased the problems by continuously keeping public housing officials on the defensive with charges of building "luxury" apartments for low-income families and of conducting a "socialistic" program. Maximum cost ceilings have prevented imaginative construction and have produced, all too often, barrackslike architecture. The resulting institutionalized atmosphere has discouraged the inhabitants from considering the "project" as "home." Also, to prevent the rapid degeneration of the housing project into a public-built slum, the local housing authorities have been forced to impose seemingly endless lists of regulations, which quite naturally create hostility between residents and the authority.[13]

These rigid regulations have had another effect on the dwellers in public housing. While public housing may, in theory, free the low-income family from the tyranny of the slums, ironically it has, in practice, created a tyranny of its own. The requirement that only persons earning less than a prescribed annual income be accepted as tenants has meant that the more ambitious residents have to leave when their incomes rise above the limit. Such a policy has deprived the projects of potential leadership. The weekly unannounced inspections to ascertain cleanliness, the snooping into bank accounts, the strict, often petty, restrictions forbidding even minor remodeling, the arbitrary evictions, and the general institutionalized atmosphere have prevented the development of a normal, stable social order and have frequently chased away the most desirable residents. "Life in the usual public housing projects," Catharine Bauer points out, "just is not the way most American families want to live. Nor does it reflect our accepted values as to the way people should live."[14]

Because public housing can accept only low-income families, other problems are created. As devised and conducted, the public housing program lies outside of the mainstream of the American experience. Whereas social security and unemployment insurance, for example, have been readily assimilated into American life, public housing has been generally rejected. The ideal of private home ownership has remained a major facet of the American way of life. Since most residents view public housing as only a stop-gap measure, pride of ownership, or even pride in renting an apartment of one's choosing, is absent.[15] The stigma of inferiority is placed upon the project dweller; his self-respect is often undermined merely by the fact that he has to accept public assistance. The myriad of regulations often complete the destruction of his own sense of individualism. Because of the low-income requirement public housing has also produced "segregation by income"—a form of social segregation based upon poverty; the physical arrangement of the typical project tends to erect a barrier between the residents and the rest of the city.[16] The new ghettos, Salisbury suggests, are equally as bad as any other form of segregation in a free society.[17]

The relativism of modern American liberalism, which Eric Goldman has so perceptively criticized,[18] enabled the reformers to justify the illiberalism of public housing with the argument that it was better than slums. By using this pragmatic, "ends justifies the means" argument, however, the public housing advocate neatly trapped himself. He failed to realize that quite often the methods employed preclude any success in reaching the desired goal. In this instance, as long as the ideals of individualism and freedom of choice evoke an enthusiastic response in America, public housing, as now constituted, will conflict with these ideals and therefore prevent any widespread success.

As discontent with public housing grew during the years after Truman's departure from office, the entire emphasis toward urban problems was slowly altered. Slum clearance became divorced from public housing and thereby gained new friends, although many cities rejected federal aid as an unwanted invasion of local affairs. But, nonetheless, slum clearance and urban renewal (the Eisenhower program of revitalizing deteriorated areas before complete clearance is needed) have played an important role in the reconstruction of over six hundred cities.[19] Public housing, however, has limped along in "a kind of limbo, continuously controversial, not dead but never more than half alive."[20] To be sure, the Housing Act of 1961 contained provisions for 100,000 units of public housing, and the Housing Act of 1965 also contained ample public housing authorizations. But in the face of the magnitude of the housing problem, these were little more than token measures. The 1965 legislation contained provisions for rent subsidies for about 375,000 low-income families, and this new approach to low-rent housing demonstrates the desire of housing officials to find a workable alternative to public housing.

The Fair Deal failed to end the long-enduring problems of slum housing; perhaps the real significance of its efforts is that the basic problems were brought into sharp focus. Poor housing results from lack of education, low income, and a general inability of impoverished groups to keep step with cultural advancement. As American life in the twentieth century became increasingly more technical, the gulf between the poor and the rest of society widened. Public housing merely helps to alleviate the product of these complex factors and does not attack the source. Only sufficient education and opportunities for employment at adequate wages will enable today's slum dwellers to enjoy the benefits of decent housing.

Nonetheless, Harry S Truman made a concerted effort to solve the housing dilemma and was the first President to recognize clearly the importance of socially sound and economically healthy cities. Although the elimination of slums and substandard housing was not even approached, the adoption of the goal, "a decent house in a good environment for every American family," was in itself a signal accomplishment.

Notes

INTRODUCTION

1. Eric Goldman, *The Crucial Decade and After, America 1945-1960*, 62-90.
2. Eric Hodgins, *Mr. Blandings Builds His Dream House.*
3. Quoted in Paul Wendt, *Housing Policy—the Search for Solutions*, 148.
4. John Keats, *The Crack in the Picture Window*, xi-xviii.

CHAPTER I

1. Art Gallaher, in *Plainville Fifteen Years Later*, Arthur Vidich and Joseph Bensman, in *Small Town in Mass Society; Class, Power, and Religion in a Rural Community*, and Lewis E. Atherton, in *Main Street on the Middle Border*, discuss the convergence of rural and urban values in American society in the twentieth century.
2. Samuel J. Eldersveld, "The Influence of Metropolitan Party Pluralities in Presidential Elections Since 1920: A Study of Twelve Key Cities," *The American Political Science Review*, XLIII (December, 1949), 1189-1206; Samuel Lubell, *The Future of American Politics*, 28-57; Walter Johnson, *1600 Pennsylvania Avenue*, 90-92, 169-70. For a concise analysis of the impact of the urban vote upon modern politics, see Carl N. Degler, "American Political

144 HOUSING REFORM DURING THE TRUMAN ADMINISTRATION

144 HOUSING REFORM DURING THE TRUMAN ADMINISTRATION

Parties and the Rise of the City: An Interpretation," *Journal of American History*, LI (June, 1964), 41-59.

3. J. Joseph Huthmacher, "Urban Liberalism and the Age of Reform," *Mississippi Valley Historical Review*, XLIX (September, 1962), 231-41.

4. *Ibid.*, 235-38.

5. For a brief but perceptive analysis of the role of urbanism in recasting the "liberal" and "conservative" programs, see Alan P. Grimes, *Equality in America: Religion, Race and the Urban Majority*, 89-126.

6. Robert Bremner, *From the Depths*, 16-19; Harry C. Bredemeier, "The Federal Public Housing Movement," unpublished doctoral dissertation, Columbia University, 9; Timothy McDonnell, *The Wagner Housing Act*, 1-3.

7. Bremner, *From the Depths*, 228-29; Roy Lubove, *The Progressives and the Slums; Tenement House Reform in New York City, 1890-1917.*

8. Lubove, *The Progressives and the Slums*; McDonnell, *The Wagner Housing Act*, 3-7; Bremner, *From the Depths*, 204-12; John G. Hill, "Fifty Years of Social Action on the Housing Front," *Social Service Review*, XXII (June, 1948), 160-76; Bredemeier, "The Federal Public Housing Movement," 24-25.

9. George Herbert Gray, *Housing and Citizenship*, 11-13; Henry S. Churchill, *The City is the People*, 71-83.

10. Bredemeier, "The Federal Public Housing Movement," 24-25, 31; Ira S. Robbins, "Housing Goals and Achievements in the United States," *American Journal of Economics and Sociology*, XV (April, 1956), 286.

11. Roy Lubove, "Homes and 'A Few Well Placed Fruit Trees': An Object Lesson in Federal Housing," *Social Research*, XXVII (Winter, 1960), 469-86.

12. Clarke A. Chambers, *Seedtime of Reform; American Social Service and Social Action, 1918-1933*, 133-38; Roy Lubove, "New Cities for Old: The Urban Reconstruction Program of the 1930's," *Social Studies*, LIII (November, 1962), 203-13; McDonnell, *The Wagner Housing Act*, 11-25; Roy Lubove, *Community Planning in the 1920's: The Contribution of the Regional Planning Association of America*, 49-66.

13. Paul F. Wendt, *Housing Policy—the Search for Solutions*, 148-52.

14. *Ibid.*, 147-48; McDonnell, *The Wagner Housing Act*, 26-28.

15. Wendt, *Housing Policy—the Search for Solutions*, 148-52; McDonnell, *The Wagner Housing Act*, 29-50.

16. Robert Moore Fisher, *Twenty Years of Public Housing*, 79-91.

17. Paul Conkin, *Tomorrow a New World: The New Deal Community Program*, 305-25.

18. Quoted in McDonnell, *The Wagner Housing Act*, 250.

19. McDonnell, *The Wagner Housing Act*, 53, 186-88; William E. Leuchtenburg, *Franklin D. Roosevelt and the New Deal, 1932-1940*, 134-36.

20. Fisher, *Twenty Years of Public Housing*, 122; McDonnell, *The Wagner Housing Act*, 135-36, 176; Bredemeier, "The Federal Public Housing Act," 87-90; Samuel E. Trotter, "A Study of Public Housing in the United States," unpublished doctoral dissertation, University of Alabama, 248.

21. *Historical Statistics of the United States, Colonial Times to 1957*, 393.

22. Fisher, *Twenty Years of Public Housing*, 208.

23. Leuchtenburg, *Franklin D. Roosevelt and the New Deal*, 136.

CHAPTER II

1. John B. Blandford, Jr., "Speech to the National Association of Housing Officials," *American City*, LVIII (June, 1943), 58.

2. Max G. Mercer, "That Postwar Dream House," *Antioch Review*, III (December, 1943), 558-73; Thomas S. Holden, "How Many Postwar Houses?" *Architectural Record*, XCIV (September, 1943), 50-51 ff.; Guy Greer, "Getting Ready for Federal Aid in Urban Redevelopment," *American City*, LVIII (May, 1943), 47-49; "A Decent Home for Every Family," *American City*, LIX (July, 1944), 91; "Where We Stand Today in Housing," *American City*, LX (February, 1945), 70; Boydon Sparkes, "Can the Cities Come Back?" *Saturday Evening Post*, CCXVII (November 4, 1944), 28 ff.; Harry Binsse, "A Place to Lay Your Head," *Commonweal*, XXXIX (December 31, 1943), 270-73; Alvin Hansen, "Urban Redevelopment," *Survey Graphic*, XXXIII (April, 1944), 204; George H. Gray, "Public Housing, a Function of Democracy," *Architectural Record*, XCIV (September, 1943), 52-53; Charles Abrams, "Government and Housing," *Nation*, CLIX (October 21, 1944), 498; Guy Greer, "Housing: The Why of Planning," *Fortune*, XXX (November, 1944), 146-51; "Housing, War and Postwar," *Survey*, LXXIX (March, 1943), 84; Loula D. Lasker, "The Call of Our Cities," *Survey Graphic*, XXXIII (April, 1944), 197-98; Ira S. Robbins, "Slums are Like Treadmills," *Survey Graphic*, XXXIII (April, 1944), 207; Dorothy Rosenman, "A Truce Upon Your Housing," *Survey Graphic*, XXXIII (January, 1944), 20-22.

3. Paul Wendt, *Housing Policy—the Search for Solutions*, 152-57; Samuel E. Trotter, "A Study of Public Housing in the United States," unpublished doctoral dissertation, University of Alabama, 163.

4. Timothy McDonnell, *The Wagner Housing Act*, 29-50;

Wendt, *Housing Policy—the Search for Solutions,* 148-52; Glenn H. Beyer, *Housing: A Factual Analysis,* 239-46.

5. Harry C. Bates, "Homes for the Future," *American Federationist,* LI (June, 1944), 9-11.

6. Typed list of organizations supporting the Wagner-Ellender-Taft housing bill, January 17, 1946, Harry S Truman Papers, OF 63; *New York Times,* January, 1943, to August, 1945, *passim;* "New York's Housing Week," *American City,* LIX (June, 1944), 95-97; Bernard B. Smith, "Those Postwar Houses?" *Harper's,* CLXXXVII (July, 1943), 108-14; "Fight on Housing," *Business Week* (December 30, 1944), 21-22; Sparkes, "Can the Cities Come Back?" *op. cit.*

7. "New York's Housing Week," *American City,* LIX (June, 1944), 95-97; *New York Times,* December 4 and 12, 1943; Nathan Straus, *The Seven Myths of Housing;* Dorothy Rosenman, *A Million Homes a Year;* R. J. Thomas, "Labor Views," *Survey Graphic,* XXXIII (April, 1944), 212; Bates, "Homes for the Future," *op. cit.*

8. Alvin Hansen, *op. cit.;* Greer, "Getting Ready for Federal Aid in Urban Redevelopment," 47-49; Rosenman, *A Million Homes a Year,* 194-217.

9. John G. Hill, "Fifty Years of Social Action on the Housing Front," *Social Service Review,* XXII (June, 1948), 176-77; Robert Bremner, *From the Depths,* 212.

10. McDonnell, *The Wagner Housing Act,* 29; Clarke A. Chambers, *Seedtime of Reform: American Social Service and Social Action, 1918-1933,* 133-38.

11. Straus, *Seven Myths of Housing,* 29-197; Charles Abrams, *The Future of Housing,* 19-35.

12. Wagner, typed copy of undated speech, Robert F. Wagner Papers.

13. B. J. Hovde, "Housing for the Low Income Group," *Journal of Home Economics,* XXXVI (April, 1944), 208; Philip N. Klutznick, "A Decent Home for Every Family," *American City,* LIX (July, 1944), 91; Abrams, "Government and Housing," 498; Rosenman, *A Million Homes a Year,* 18-46; Straus, *Seven Myths of Housing,* 145-63.

14. U.S., Congress, Senate, Special Committee on Postwar Economic Policy and Planning, Subcommittee on Housing and Urban Redevelopment, *Hearings Pursuant to S. Res. 102 (78th Cong.),* 79th Cong., 1st Sess., January 16, 1945, 1708.

15. *Ibid.,* January 11, 1945, 1572.

16. *Ibid.,* January 16, 1945, 1744, testimony of Bleeker Marquette, representative of the National Association of Housing Officials.

17. Harry C. Bredemeier, "The Federal Public Housing Movement," unpublished doctoral dissertation, Columbia University, 214.

18. *New York Times*, March 8, 9, 10, and 11, 1944, reports the events at the Chicago meeting, where members of the housing industry discussed postwar housing with leaders of the housing reform movement. The meeting ended in complete disagreement over public housing. For a full report of the meeting, see *Survey Graphic*, XXXIII (April, 1944), 196-213.

19. Ira S. Robbins, "Housing Goals and Achievements in the United States," *American Journal of Economics and Sociology*, XV (April, 1956), 290; "Public Housing in the Doldrums," *New Republic*, CX (May 1, 1944), 595-96; Abrams, *The Future of Housing*, 323; Charles Abrams, "Homeless America," *Nation*, CLXIII (December 28, 1946), 755.

20. Karl Schriftgiesser, *The Lobbyists*, 218.

21. *Ibid.*, 216-23; Bredemeier, "The Federal Public Housing Movement," 146.

22. *Ibid.*, 142-43.

23. *Historical Statistics of the United States, Colonial Times to 1957*, 393.

24. Wendt, *Housing Policy—the Search for Solutions*, 148-52.

25. Richard S. Kirkendall, "The Great Depression: Another Watershed in American History?" in John Braeman, Robert H. Bremner, and Everett Walters, eds., *Change and Continuity in Twentieth-Century America*, 174-84.

26. Bredemeier, "The Federal Public Housing Movement," 147; Wendt, *Housing Policy—the Search for Solutions*, 148-52.

27. Bredemeier, "The Federal Public Housing Movement," 142-43.

28. *Ibid.*, 141.

29. *Ibid.*, 147.

30. Testimony of Herbert U. Nelson, executive vice-president of the National Association of Real Estate Boards, Senate, Subcommittee on Housing and Urban Redevelopment, *Hearings*, February 6, 1945, 2004-5, 2018.

31. Quoted in Abrams, "Homeless America," 754.

32. Bredemeier, "The Federal Public Housing Movement," 147.

33. Herbert U. Nelson, Speech before the American Legion Housing Committee, reported in *New York Times*, November 8, 1946; Morton Fitch, president of the National Association of Real Estate Boards, quoted in *New York Times*, March 28, 1947.

34. *Headlines*, XVI (June 20 and 27, 1949).

35. Nelson testimony, Senate, Subcommittee on Housing and Urban Redevelopment, *Hearings*, February 6, 1945, 2004-21.

36. Senate, Subcommittee on Housing and Urban Redevelopment, *Hearings*, 1944.

37. Douglas Whitlock, president of the Producers' Council, Senate, Subcommittee on Housing and Urban Redevelopment,

Hearings, 1993-94, and H. R. Northrup, secretary-manager of the National Retail Lumber Dealers Association, 2000-2003.

38. Earl Bryan Schwust, executive vice-president of the Bowery Savings Bank of New York City, Senate, Subcommittee on Housing and Urban Redevelopment, *Hearings,* 1959-60.

39. Senate, Subcommittee on Housing and Urban Redevelopment, *Hearings,* 1933.

40. *Headlines,* XII (July 9, 1945).

41. Joseph E. Merrion, Senate, Subcommittee on Housing and Urban Redevelopment, *Hearings,* February 7, 1945, 2084.

42. *Ibid.,* 2080.

43. *Headlines,* XII (November 19, 1945).

44. Seward H. Mott, director of the Urban Land Institute, Senate, Subcommittee on Housing and Urban Redevelopment, *Hearings,* January 12, 1945, 1593-1604.

45. Robert M. Fisher, *Twenty Years of Public Housing,* 208.

46. Nelson, Senate, Subcommittee on Housing and Urban Redevelopment, *Hearings,* February 6, 1945, 2020.

47. Schriftgiesser, *The Lobbyists,* 216-23.

48. Wendt, *Housing Policy—the Search For Solutions,* 180-84.

49. John Keats, *The Crack in the Picture Window,* xi-xvii; editors of *Fortune, The Exploding Metropolis,* 115-39.

50. U.S., *Congressional Record,* 78th Cong., 1st Sess., March 12, 1943, 1922.

51. Eric Goldman, *Rendezvous with Destiny,* 300.

52. Charles E. Merriam, "The National Resources Planning Board: A Chapter in American Planning Experience," *American Political Science Review,* XXXVIII (December, 1944), 1084; "Planning and Politics," *Nation,* CLVI (March 20, 1943), 405-7; *New York Times,* February 16 and 27, 1943; "Canning the Planners," *Commonweal,* XXXVIII (June 11, 1943), 192.

53. *Congressional Record,* 78th Cong., 1st Sess., February 8, 1943, 721.

54. *Ibid.,* March 15, 1943, 1977.

55. "Planning and Politics," *Nation, op. cit.*

56. Samuel I. Rosenman, ed., *The Public Papers of Franklin D. Roosevelt, 1943,* 99.

57. Press conference, *Public Papers of Franklin D. Roosevelt, 1943,* 143.

58. *Congressional Record,* 78th Cong., 1st Sess., March 12, 1943, 1922.

59. *Ibid.,* February 15, 1943, 900.

60. "Canning the Planners," *Commonweal, op. cit.*

61. *Ibid.*

62. Franklin D. Roosevelt, in a letter to Dorothy Rosenman, chairman of the National Committee on Housing, printed in *New York Times,* March 9, 1944.

63. *Public Papers of Franklin D. Roosevelt, 1944,* 41.

64. John B. Blandford, Jr., Senate, Subcommittee on Housing and Urban Redevelopment, *Hearings,* January 9, 1945, 1325.

65. Senate, Subcommittee on Housing and Urban Redevelopment, *Hearings, passim.*

66. *Ibid.*

67. U.S., Congress, Senate, Special Committee on Postwar Economic Policy and Planning, Subcommittee on Housing and Urban Redevelopment, Report, 79th Cong., 1st Sess., August 1, 1945, 23; *Congressional Record,* 79th Cong., 1st Sess., August 1, 1945, 8237-44.

68. Senate, Subcommittee on Housing and Urban Redevelopment, Report, *passim.*

69. *Ibid.,* 6-7.

CHAPTER III

1. Paul Wendt, *Housing Policy—the Search for Solutions,* 148-52; William E. Leuchtenburg, *Franklin D. Roosevelt and the New Deal, 1932-1940,* 134-36.

2. Norman Podhoretz, "Truman and the Idea of the Common Man," *Commentary,* XXI (May, 1956), 469-74.

3. Jonathan Daniels, *The Man of Independence,* 95-101, 121-22; Edward R. Schauffler, *Harry Truman, Son of the Soil,* 55; Cyril Clemens, *The Man From Missouri,* 210-16.

4. Daniels, *The Man of Independence,* 105-9; Harry S Truman, *Memoirs,* Vol. I, *Year of Decisions,* 123.

5. Eugene F. Schmidtlein, "Truman the Senator," unpublished doctoral dissertation, University of Missouri, 40-41.

6. *Ibid.,* 218.

7. *Ibid.,* 1, 52, 331; Eugene F. Schmidtlein, "Truman's First Senatorial Election," *Missouri Historical Review,* LVII (January, 1963), 138, 152-53; Truman, *Year of Decisions,* 143.

8. Schmidtlein, "Truman the Senator," 118, 260-61, 272; Daniel P. Parker, "Political and Social Views of Harry S Truman," unpublished doctoral dissertation, University of Pennsylvania, 46; Harry S Truman, "A Plan for the Regional Developments of Tomorrow," *Civil Engineering,* XIV (November, 1944), 465.

9. Truman, Message to Congress, September 6, 1945, Truman Papers, PPF 200.

10. Truman, *Year of Decisions,* 482.

11. Truman, Message to Congress, September 6, 1945, Truman Papers, PPF 200.

12. Truman, *Year of Decisions,* 483; Joe Martin, *My First Fifty Years in Politics,* 177-78.

13. Daniels, *Man of Independence,* 297.

14. Martin, *My First Fifty Years in Politics,* 177-78.

15. U.S., *Congressional Record,* 79th Cong., 1st Sess., November 14, 1945, 10642-52.

16. *Congressional Record,* 77th Cong., 2nd Sess., February 25, 1942, 1596.

17. Ethel Gunnison Youngblood, "The Position of Robert A. Taft on the Housing Issue," unpublished Master's thesis, University of Connecticut, 18.

18. *Ibid.; Congressional Record,* 77th Cong., 2nd Sess., February 25, 1942, 1596; Robert A. Taft, Speech before the Better Housing League of Cincinnati, October 30, 1943, in *Congressional Record,* 78th Cong., 1st Sess., November 16, 1943, A4892-93; "Toward Unity in Postwar Housing," 11-14; William S. White, *The Taft Story,* 41-52.

19. Taft, Speech before the National Public Housing Conference, June 19, 1945, reprinted in "Toward Unity in Postwar Housing," 11-14; Youngblood, "The Position of Robert A. Taft on the Housing Issue," 14; Taft, Speech to the National Association of Housing Officials, February 24, 1943, in *Congressional Record,* 78th Cong., 1st Sess., March 1, 1943, A839-40.

20. White, *The Taft Story,* 52.

21. *Current Biography, 1946,* 178-80; Allan P. Sindler, *Huey Long's Louisiana,* 214-17.

22. Robert F. Wagner to Lee F. Johnson, executive vice-president of the National Public Housing Conference, March 24, 1944, Robert F. Wagner Papers.

23. *Congressional Record,* 79th Cong., 1st Sess., November 14, 1945, 10644; Sindler, *Huey Long's Louisiana,* 204; V. O. Key, *Southern Politics in State and Nation,* 162.

24. Key, *Southern Politics in State and Nation,* 377-78; Alexander Heard, *A Two-Party South?,* 152-54. See also Dewey Grantham, *The Democratic South,* 69-80, for an excellent analysis of the "conservative-liberal" split in Southern politics.

25. *Current Biography, 1941,* 892-94.

26. Wagner, Speech at Westchester, New York, November 1, 1944, Wagner Papers.

27. Speech before the National Public Housing Conference, June 19, 1945, in *Congressional Record,* 79th Cong., 1st Sess., June 21, 1945, A2973; Wagner to Senator James E. Murray, March 7, 1945; Speech before the Metropolitan League of Savings and Loan Associations, New York City, October 19, 1944, Wagner Papers; Wagner to the Home Building Committee, November 15, 1945, Wagner Papers.

28. Wagner, press release, October 29, 1945; Speech before the Metropolitan League of Savings and Loan Associations, *op. cit.;* Speech before the National Public Housing Conference, *op. cit.*

29. *Congressional Record,* 79th Cong., 1st Sess., November 14, 1945, 10642.

30. *Ibid.,* 10644.

31. *Ibid.,* 10652-53.

32. Raymond M. Foley, administrator of the Housing and Home Finance Agency, 1947-1953, says that this was the strategy used by the Truman Administration in order to get public housing accepted. Interview, July 25, 1961, Washington, D. C.

33. *Headlines,* XII (June 25, 1945).

34. *Ibid.,* November 19, 1945.

35. *Ibid.,* December 3, 1945.

CHAPTER IV

1. Joseph M. Stack, commander-in-chief of the Veterans of Foreign Wars, to Harry S Truman, December 14, 1945, Harry S Truman Papers, OF 63.

2. Eric Goldman, *The Crucial Decade and After, America 1945-1960,* 26; Samuel E. Trotter, "A Study of Public Housing in the United States," unpublished doctoral dissertation, University of Alabama, 180; Bill Mauldin, *Back Home,* 61-68; Charles Abrams, "Homeless America," *Nation,* CLXIII (December 21 and 28, 1946), 723-25, 753-55; "Mr. Wyatt's Housing Shortage," *Fortune,* XXXIII (April, 1946), 105-9; *Time,* XLVII (April 8, 1946), 23; *U.S. News & World Report,* XX (May 8, 1946), 30-31.

3. John W. Snyder, director of the Office of War Mobilization and Reconversion, memorandum to Truman, December 3, 1945, Congressman Clarence Cannon to Truman, January 4, 1946, Senator Hugh Mitchell to Truman, January 4, 1946, Congressman Jerry Voorhis to Truman, December 5, 1945, Thomas B. Monk, mayor of Sacramento, to Truman, November 24, 1945, Woodall Rodgers, mayor of Dallas, to Truman, November 1, 1945, Jack Hardy, national commander of AMVETS, to Truman, December 7, 1945, Milton Eisenhower, president of Kansas State University, to Truman, November 13, 1945, R. J. Thomas, housing chairman, UAW-CIO to Truman, November 13, 1945, and September 14, 1945, Nathan Straus, former administrator of the Federal Public Housing Agency, to Truman, January 4, 1946, Congressman George H. Fallon to Truman, December 3, 1945, Truman Papers, OF 63. *New York Times,* December 9, 1945, VIII; *Time,* XLVI (October 22 and December 24, 1945), 21, 22-23; *Life,* XIX (December 17, 1945), 27-36; Ralph G. Martin, "Homes for Veterans," *New Republic,* CXIII (December 10, 1945), 791-93.

4. *Current Biography,* 1945, 561-64.

5. *New York Times Magazine,* September 23, 1945, 13; *Current Biography,* 1945, 562-63.

6. Tris Coffin, *Missouri Compromise*, 31; *New York Times Magazine*, September 23, 1945, 13.

7. John W. Snyder, director of Office of War Mobilization and Reconversion, memorandum to Truman, "A Program to Stimulate Housing," September 18, 1945, Truman Papers, OF 133; Wilson Wyatt, Speech to the Twenty-eighth American Legion Convention, October 3, 1946, San Francisco, Speech File, Office of Housing Expediter Papers.

8. John W. Snyder, memorandum to Truman, "Report on Housing," December 12, 1945, Truman Papers, OF 122-I; Harry S Truman, *Memoirs*, Vol. I, *Year of Decisions*, 512-13; *New York Times*, December 13, 1945.

9. George E. Allen, *Presidents Who Have Known Me*, 208; Truman to Wyatt, December 12, 1946, Truman Papers, OF 63; *Newsweek*, XXVII (January 21, 1946), 37.

10. *New York Times*, January 26, 1946.

11. Truman, radio address to the nation, "On the Status of Reconversion," January 3, 1946, in Harry S Truman, *Public Papers of the Presidents, Harry S Truman, 1946*, 7; Wilson Wyatt, press release, January 5, 1946, Truman Papers, OF 63.

12. Wilson Wyatt, "Report of the Housing Expediter," February 8, 1946, and Truman, "Statement Upon the Release of the Veterans' Emergency Housing Program," February 8, 1946, Truman Papers, OF 63. The remainder of the report concerned conversion of war defense housing to temporary housing for veterans, conversion of war factories to prefabricated housing plants, training of 1,500,000 men to work in the home-building industry, liberalization of Federal Housing Administration mortgage insurance terms, and the enactment of the Wagner-Ellender-Taft bill to carry on the program after the termination of the VEHP on December 31, 1947.

13. Wyatt, "Report of the Housing Expediter," February 8, 1946, Truman Papers, OF 63.

14. The extensive debates are recorded in U.S., *Congressional Record*, 79th Cong., 2nd Sess., March 1, 1946, 1829-48; March 4, 1863-91; March 5, 1940-64, and March 6, 1974-95.

15. Wyatt, telegram to Truman, February 27, 1946, and Truman to Sam Rayburn, March 1, 1946, Truman Papers, OF 63; Wyatt, quoted in *The New York Times*, March 4, 1946; Truman, Speech at the Jackson Day Dinner, March 23, 1946, in Truman, *Public Papers*, 167-68; Truman, transcript of press conference, Records of the White House Reporter, March 28, 1946, Truman Papers, 11; *Congressional Record*, 79th Cong., 2nd Sess., March 7, 1946, 2001.

16. *Congressional Record*, 79th Cong., 2nd Sess., April 10, 1946, 3433; May 13, 4915, 4939; *New York Times*, April 10 and 11, May 13, 14, and 23, 1946.

17. *Congressional Record*, 79th Cong., 2nd Sess., April 15, 1946, 3701.

18. Truman, "Veto of the Price Control Bill," in Truman, *Public Papers*, June 29, 1946, 332.

19. Wyatt, "Speech to the Nation," July 1, 1946, Speech File, Housing Expediter Papers; Truman, "Special Message to Congress on Signing the Second Price Control Bill," July 25, 1946, in Truman, *Public Papers*, 359-62; *New York Times*, July 2, 19, and 26, 1946.

20. *Current Biography*, *1949*, 640-42; *Newsweek*, XXVII (February 18, 1946), 37; Timothy McDonnell, *The Wagner Housing Act*, 366.

21. Raymond Foley to John Steelman, June 17, 1946, Truman Papers, OF 63; *Current Biography*, *1949*, 641-42; "Housing: Poor Hope," *New Republic*, CXV (December 9, 1946), 749; "Housing Bill is Shelved," *American Federationist*, LIII (August, 1946), 15-28.

22. *Congressional Digest*, XXV (November, 1946), 261; Speeches in the House of Representatives, recorded in *Congressional Record*, 79th Cong., 2nd Sess.: Brent Spence, July 26, 1946, 10188, and Charles R. Savage, July 31, 1946, A4934.

23. Foley to Steelman, June 17, 1946, Truman Papers, OF 63; *New York Times*, July 4, 23, 25, 28, and 31, 1946.

24. Wilson Wyatt, Speeches before AFL Conference, in Asheville, North Carolina, May 11, 1946, before Buffalo, New York, Chamber of Commerce, June 5, 1946; before the Citizens Council for Community Planning, June 17, 1946, Speech File, Housing Expediter Papers; *New York Times*, July 23, 26, and 28, 1946.

25. Truman to Spence, July 25, 1946, Truman Papers, OF 63.

26. Truman to McCormack, Truman to Rayburn, July 25, 1946, Truman Papers, OF 63.

27. *Congressional Digest*, XXV (November, 1946), 261; "Housing Bill is Shelved," *American Federationist*, LIII (August, 1946), 28.

28. *New York Times*, July 31, 1946; *Headlines*, XIII (August 5, 1946), 1.

29. *New York Times*, March 27, 1946; *Newsweek*, XXVII (April 8, 1946), 66; *Time*, XLVII (April 8, 1946), 22-23.

30. "The Promise of the Shortage," *Fortune*, XXXIII (April, 1946), 102. See also the following for discussions of the problems existing within the building industry at this time: Robert Lasch, *Breaking the Building Blockade*, 81-113; Dorothy Rosenman, *A Million Homes a Year*, 48-77; Nat Rogg, *A History of the Veterans' Emergency Housing Program*, 9; "Mr. Wyatt Builds His Castle," *Fortune*, XXXIV (July, 1946), 3; Marjorie Foulkrod, "Case History of Housing," *Current History*, XV (September, 1948), 138-43.

31. "Mr. Wyatt Builds His Castle," *Fortune, op. cit.*; Truman, *Year of Decisions*, 515; Truman, "Radio Address to the American

People on the Railroad Strike Emergency," May 24, 1946, in Truman, *Public Papers,* 276; *Time,* XLVI (December 24, 1945), 22-23; *New York Times,* May 23, 1946.

32. *New York Times,* July 14, August 7 and 14, and October 1, 1946; "The Housing Mess," *Fortune,* XXXV (January, 1947), 81; Frank McNaughton and Walter Hehmeyer, *Harry Truman, President,* 215; Paul F. Wendt, *The Role of the Federal Government in Housing,* 7; Robert C. Weaver, *The Negro Ghetto,* 309; *New York Times,* September 1, 1946; *Time,* XLVIII (December 24, 1946), 24; Senator Glen H. Taylor to Truman, November 26, 1946, Congressman Frank A. Matthews to Truman, November 16, 1946, Truman Papers, OF 63.

33. *Headlines,* XIII (February 25, 1946); "Crow's Weekly Letter," confidential letter of the Northwest Lumber Industry, August 9, 1946, in Truman Papers, OF 63; Newton Farr, president of the National Association of Real Estate Boards, quoted in *The New York Times,* October 3, 1946; resolution to Harry S Truman from the Construction League of Indianapolis, October 4, 1946; E. W. Spriggs, president of the Indianapolis Real Estate Board to Truman, October 3, 1946, Senator W. Lee O'Daniel to Truman, October 28, 1946, Truman Papers, OF 63. A great amount of such material as this is in the Truman Papers, OF 63. This campaign is best treated in Bryant Putney, "Obituary for Veterans' Housing," *Nation,* CLXIII (December 21, 1946), 722-23, and more generally in Karl Schriftgiesser, *The Lobbyists,* Chap. 14; Mauldin, *Back Home,* gives the viewpoint of a veteran who was very critical of the activities of the real estate lobby.

34. Paul H. Griffith, national commander of the American Legion, to Truman, December 7, 1946, Truman Papers, OF 333-misc.; memorandum to William Hassett, White House aide, based upon a telephone call from Ray Sawyer, national commander of the American Veterans of World War II, November 27, 1946, and Louis Starr, commander-in-chief of the Veterans of Foreign Wars, to Truman, November 13, 1946, Truman Papers, OF 63. Each veterans' group leader praised Wyatt's efforts, but pointed out that the promised housing was not available. See also "Report of the Special National Committee on Veterans' Housing of the American Legion," November 22, 1946, Truman Papers, OF 63; *New York Times,* October 4 and 20, November 23 and 25, 1946.

35. *Current Biography, 1946,* 559-60; *U.S. News & World Report,* XX (February 8, 1946), 65-66.

36. *U.S. News & World Report,* XXI (October 18, 1946), 19; *New York Times,* September 1 and 21, 1946.

37. John D. Small, memorandum to Clark Clifford, December 3, 1946, Clark Clifford Papers.

38. *New York Times,* October 26, November 3 and 5, 1946.

39. *Current Biography, 1946,* 12-14; *U.S. News & World Report,* XX (February 15, 1946), 66-67; Coffin, *Missouri Compromise,* 32-33.

40. McNaughton and Hehmeyer, *Harry Truman, President,* 214-15; "Shambles," *New Republic,* CXV (December 16, 1946), 791; *Time,* XLVIII (November 25 and December 9, 1946), 89, 24; Wilson Wyatt, Speech before the Special Committee to Investigate the National Defense, November 25, 1946, Housing Expediter Papers; Wyatt to Matthew Connelly, presidential secretary, November 22, 1946, Truman Papers, OF 63; *New York Times,* November 2, 13, and 26, 1946.

41. *Time,* XLVIII (December 9, 1946), 24; *U.S. News & World Report,* XXI (October 25, 1946), 26; *New York Times,* November 13, 1946. Nathan Straus, former administrator of the Federal Public Housing Agency under Franklin D. Roosevelt, was very critical of Wyatt's reliance upon the prefabrication industry. Straus pointed out that the industry never produced over 50,000 houses in any single year during the Truman Administration (Straus, *Two-Thirds of a Nation; A Housing Program,* 57-65). On November 25, 1946, Allen surprised Wyatt by approving the loans for the ten other companies (totalling $38 million), but refused to grant a loan to Lustron.

42. "Statement by the President Terminating Price and Wage Controls," November 9, 1946, in Truman, *Public Papers,* 475-77.

43. *Ibid.*

44. *New York Times,* February 24, 1946.

45. Tris Coffin, *Missouri Compromise,* 31; *New York Times,* June 2 and 6, 1946.

46. Harry S Truman, *Year of Decisions,* 483-84.

47. *Current Biography, 1941,* 818-19; Tris Coffin, "John Steelman," *New Republic,* CXV (November 11, 1946), 625-26; *Newsweek,* XXVII (September 21, 1946), 25.

48. Coffin, *Missouri Compromise,* 43-44; *Current Biography, 1941,* 819; Charles A. Madison, *Leaders and Liberals in 20th Century America,* 433.

49. "The Shape of Things," *Nation,* CLXIII (November 16, 1946), 541; *New Republic,* CXV (November 18, 1946), 659.

50. Wilson Wyatt, Radio Speech over the Mutual Broadcasting System, November 14, 1946, Speech File, Housing Expediter Papers; Wyatt to Edwin G. Nourse, chairman of the Council of Economic Advisers, November 27, 1946, Housing Expediter Papers.

51. Wyatt, memorandum to Truman, November 27, 1946, Truman Papers, OF 122-I; Report of the Housing Expediter for 1947, Truman Papers, OF 63.

52. Small, memorandum to Clifford, December 3, 1946, Clifford Papers.

53. *New York Times*, December 4, 1946; Wyatt to Truman, December 4, 1946, Truman Papers, OF 63.

54. Truman, "Statement by the President on the Veterans' Emergency Housing Program," December 4, 1946, in Truman, *Public Papers*, 489.

55. "Statement by the President Outlining the Housing Program for 1947," December 14, 1946, in Truman, *Public Papers*, 495-98.

CHAPTER V

1. Raymond Foley to S. A. Kaye, editor of *World Biography*, January 7, 1952, Raymond M. Foley Papers.

2. Foley to Dr. James K. Pollock, member of the Commission on Organization of the Executive Branch of the Government, October 5, 1948, Foley, Speech before the United States Savings and Loan League, San Francisco, September 18, 1947, press release of testimony of Foley before the Senate Banking and Currency Committee, March 18, 1947, press release of testimony before the Joint Committee on Housing, January 20, 1948, Foley Papers. *Business Week* (September 10, 1949), in a short biographical sketch of Foley, said: "Reputation—That judgment pretty well sums up the feeling of the housing fraternity—both public and private. Fourteen years in housing posts for the government have gained Foley a reputation as a capable manager and a man unbiased as between private and public housing," clipping in Foley Papers.

3. *Business Week*, September 10, 1949, 6, clipping in Foley Papers.

4. U.S., Congress, House, Special Committee on Lobbying Activities, *Hearings*, 81st Cong., 2nd Sess., May 5, 1950, 471; copy of a Louisville, Kentucky, *Courier-Journal* story of May 6, 1950, in Foley Papers, quotes Republican Congressman Clarence Brown of Ohio as saying to Foley, upon the completion of his testimony, "You have the reputation of being the fairest, ablest, and most honest of the bureaucrats in Washington"; Oscar Kreutz to Foley, February 27, 1953, Foley Papers.

5. *Business Week*, September 10, 1949, 6, clipping in Foley Papers; interview with Foley, July 25, 1961.

6. *Ibid.*; Foley to Truman, April 13, 1948, Foley to Truman, April 27, 1948, Housing and Home Finance Agency Papers; Foley to Truman, December 30, 1952, speech draft, December 23, 1949, Foley Papers; Truman, press conference, December 15, 1949, Records of the White House Reporter, 10, Harry S Truman Papers.

7. Foley to E. W. Blum of the National Association of Housing Officials, November 10, 1947, White House File, Housing and Home Finance Agency Papers.

8. Foley, Speech before the National Association of Home Builders, Dallas, Texas, October 25, 1947, Foley Papers.

9. Foley to Pollock, October 5, 1948, Foley Papers.

10. Foley, Speech before the National Association of Home Builders, Dallas, Texas, October 24, 1947, Speech before the National Public Housing Conference, March 12, 1947, Speech before the National Association of Housing Officials, October 13, 1948, Foley Papers.

11. Samuel E. Trotter, "A Study of Public Housing in the United States," unpublished doctoral dissertation, University of Alabama, 203; *New York Times,* May 28, 1947; U.S., *Congressional Record,* 80th Cong., 1st Sess., July 22, 1947, 9653-56; Taft, Speech to Senate, *ibid.,* 9657.

12. *Ibid.,* 9961.

13. Curtis F. Scott, president of the National Savings and Loan League to Allen J. Ellender, printed in the *Congressional Record,* 80th Cong., 1st Sess., July 22, 1947, 9655-56.

14. *Congressional Record,* 80th Cong., 1st Sess., July 22, 1947, 9669.

15. *Ibid.,* 9666-67.

16. *Ibid.,* 9649-69; Foley to Walter H. Rolapp, undated letter, but obviously written shortly after the successful reorganization of the Housing and Home Finance Agency, Foley Papers; interview with Raymond M. Foley, July 25, 1961, Washington, D.C. Foley places great importance upon the permanent agency: "It set the stage for real work," he said in the interview.

17. State of the Union Address, January 7, 1947, Truman Papers, OF 419-F.

18. U.S., Senate, Committee on Banking and Currency, *Report to Accompany S. 866,* 80th Cong., 1st Sess., April 24, 1947; *New York Times,* April 24, 1947.

19. *New York Times,* January 21, March 19, May 19 and 27, and June 26, 1947; *Congressional Record,* 80th Cong., 1st Sess., March 10, 1947, 1915.

20. *Ibid.,* July 25, 1947, 10187.

21. State of the Union Address, January 7, 1947, Truman Papers, OF 419-F; press conference, January 23, 1947, Records of the White House Reporter, Truman Papers, 3.

22. A large sample of petitions, resolutions, and letters requesting the end of rent control is in Truman Papers, OF 63-A. Similar materials are in the following manuscript collections, which are open: Housing Files, Thomas C. Connally Papers; Housing Files, Wat Arnold Papers; Housing Files, William C. Cole Papers.

23. Public opinion mail urging the continuation of rent controls is in Truman Papers, OF 63-A. Among the major groups endorsing such a continuation were the following: American Federation of Labor, Congress of Industrial Organizations, Veterans

of Foreign Wars, National Conference of Catholic Churches, United States Conference of Mayors, National Public Housing Conference, National Association for Advancement of Colored People, AMVETS, and the National Association for Rural Housing. The only veterans' group opposing rent control was the American Legion.

24. Senator Glen Taylor to Truman, June 23, 1947, Truman Papers, OF 63-A; *Congressional Record*, 80th Cong., 1st Sess., June 17, 1947, 7153-60.

25. *New York Times*, June 12, 1947.

26. Frank Creedon, memorandum to F. J. Bailey, assistant director of Legislative Reference, Bureau of the Budget, June 24, 1947, Housing Bill File, Truman Papers.

27. Press release, June 30, 1947, Truman Papers, OF 63.

28. Joseph R. McCarthy, Speech in the Senate, *Congressional Record*, 80th Cong., 1st Sess., July 25, 1947, 10185; Jesse Wolcott, Speech in the House of Representatives, *ibid.*, July 24, 1947, 10080-81.

29. *Ibid.*, July 17, 1947, 9237.

30. Two books dealing with the many problems involved in housing had appeared within the previous two years: Dorothy Rosenman, *A Million Homes a Year*, and Robert Lasch, *Breaking the Building Blockade*.

31. *Congressional Record*, 80th Cong., 1st Sess., July 24, 1947, 10079-80.

32. Robert F. Wagner, press release, September 8, 1947, Robert F. Wagner Papers.

33. Richard H. Rovere, *Senator Joe McCarthy*, 107-8.

34. Members of the committee were: Senators John Sparkman (Dem., Ala.), Glen H. Taylor (Dem., Idaho), Wagner, Harry P. Cain (Rep., Wash.), Ralph Flanders (Rep., Vt.), Charles W. Tobey (Rep., N.H.), and McCarthy; Representatives Ralph A. Gamble (Rep., N.Y.), Albert Rains (Dem., Ala.), Franklin L. Sundstrom (Rep., N.J.), Rolla C. McMillen (Rep., Ill.), Charles K. Fletcher (Rep., Calif.), Wright Patman (Dem., Tex.), and Hale Boggs (Dem., La.).

35. Proxies of Wagner, Boggs, Patman, and Sparkman were rejected.

36. *New York Times*, August 20, 1947; Rovere, *Senator Joe McCarthy*, 107.

37. *New York Times*, August 20, 1947.

38. *Ibid.*

39. Robert F. Wagner, press release, September 8, 1947, Wagner Papers.

40. Nat Keith to Foley, "Memorandum on the Hearings of the Joint Committee on Housing," November 10, 1947, Foley Papers; Joseph McCarthy, "General Report," February 10, 1948, J. Howard

McGrath Papers; *New York Times,* November 4 and 21, 1947; *New York Times,* January 16, 17, and 29, 1948.
   41. Keith to Foley, November 10, 1947, Foley Papers.
   42. U.S., Congress, *Final Majority Report,* Joint Committee on Housing, March 15, 1948.
   43. Joseph R. McCarthy, "Individual Views," March 22, 1948, Truman Papers, OF 63. McCarthy charged that in many public housing developments families who were capable of paying their own rent were enjoying the benefits of government subsidy. In the *Final Majority Report,* however, the Joint Committee said that in all public housing units the average income of each family was just $1,691 in 1946; the average income for the families admitted to public housing in 1946 was $1,317.
   44. McCarthy, "Individual Views," *op. cit.,* 16.
   45. Rovere, *Senator Joe McCarthy,* 107-8.
   46. *Ibid.;* U.S., Congress, Senate, Committee on Rules and Administration, Subcommittee on Privileges and Elections, *Report,* 82nd Cong., 2nd Sess., 1952, 15-19 (Senator Thomas Hennings, chairman).
   47. *Ibid.,* 18.
   48. *Historical Statistics of the United States, Colonial Times to 1957,* 393.

CHAPTER VI

   1. Eric Goldman, *The Crucial Decade and After, America 1945-1960,* 81-83; Charles A. Madison, *Leaders and Liberals in 20th Century America,* 444-45; Jules Abels, *Out of the Jaws of Victory,* 1-88.
   2. Abels, *Out of the Jaws of Victory,* 95-96; Harry S Truman, *Memoirs,* Vol. II, *Years of Trial and Hope,* 207.
   3. Truman, *Years of Trial and Hope,* 208.
   4. *Wall Street Journal,* July 16, 1948, clipping in the Acceptance Speech File, Democratic National Committee Papers.
   5. Abels, *Out of the Jaws of Victory,* 95.
   6. Harry S Truman, Speech to the Young Democrats Club, May 14, 1948, Charles S. Murphy Files.
   7. Truman, *Years of Trial and Hope,* 211.
   8. State of the Union Message, January 7, 1948, Murphy Files; *Philadelphia Inquirer,* January 8, 1948, in State of the Union File, Democratic National Committee Papers.
   9. State of the Union Message, Murphy Files.
   10. John B. Blandford, Jr., to James Webb, director of the Budget, undated memorandum, but obviously written in early 1948, James Webb Papers; Truman to Raymond Foley, October 30, 1947, Harry S Truman Papers, OF 419-F; Truman, Speech

before the National Conference on Family Life, *New York Times,* May 7, 1948; Truman, Message to Congress, *New York Times,* April 15, 1948; Foley to Congressman Hale Boggs, June 14, 1948, Foley to Allen Ellender, April 28, 1948, Raymond M. Foley Papers.

11. Truman, Message to Congress, February 23, 1948, Truman Papers, OF 63.

12. Truman, telegram to John F. Kennedy, February 27, 1948, Truman Papers, OF 63.

13. Paul F. Wendt, *Housing Policy—the Search for Solutions,* 156.

14. *New York Times,* March 17 and 31, 1948.

15. Truman, press release, March 30, 1948, Truman Papers, OF 63-A; *New York Times,* March 31, 1948.

16. U.S., *Congressional Record,* 80th Cong., 2nd Sess., March 15, 1948, 2797.

17. *New York Times,* April 8, 1948.

18. *Congressional Record,* 80th Cong., 2nd Sess., April 14, 1948, 4411-24, April 15, 1948, 4478-4523, April 20, 1948, 4595-4618.

19. *Ibid.,* April 22, 1948, 4738.

20. Truman to Foley, April 23, 1948, Truman Papers, OF 1282.

21. Truman, Speech to Young Democrats Club, May 14, 1948, Speech File, Murphy Files.

22. "Last Chance for Houses," *New Republic,* CXIX (May 24, 1948), 8; *New York Times,* June 6 and 8, 1948.

23. *New York Times,* June 11, 1948. Republicans Merlin Hull (Wis.) and William Stratton (Ill.) joined with Scott to vote for the bill with eleven Democrats.

24. *New York Times,* June 16 and 17, 1948; Foley to Truman, Charles Ross, and Clark Clifford, Truman Papers, OF 63.

25. Republican Senator Charles Tobey indicted their role in supporting Wolcott's action in a speech on the Senate floor on August 5, 1948. The three men constituted "a triumvirate in the House," he said.

26. Ralph E. Flanders, *Senator from Vermont,* 221; *New York Times,* June 11, 1948.

27. Truman, *Years of Trial and Hope,* 175-78; Abels, *Out of the Jaws of Victory,* 38-46.

28. Truman, *Years of Trial and Hope,* 179.

29. *New York Times,* June 15 and 18, 1948; "Pre-campaign Trip File," Murphy Files, especially the speech in Los Angeles, June 14, 1948.

30. *New York Times,* June 15, 1948.

31. Abels, *Out of the Jaws of Victory,* 38; Truman, *Years of Trial and Hope,* 171-72, 175.

32. *New York Times,* June 18, 1948.

33. *Congressional Record,* 80th Cong., 2nd Sess., June 16, 1948, 8527; *New York Times,* June 17, 1948.

34. *Congressional Record,* 80th Cong., 2nd Sess., June 18, 1948, 8898; *New York Times,* June 19, 1948.

35. *Congressional Record,* 80th Cong., 2nd Sess., June 18, 1948, 8880; *New York Times,* June 19, 1948.

36. *Congressional Record,* 80th Cong., 2nd Sess., June 19, 1948, 9087. Both statements are contained on the same page.

37. Mike Monroney to Foley, June 19, 1948, Foley Papers; *New York Times,* June 19, 1948.

38. Typed copy of the Republican platform in the 1948 Platform Folder, Samuel I. Rosenman Papers.

39. Madison, *Leaders and Liberals,* 447; Abels, *Out of the Jaws of Victory,* 140-62; Dewey's discussion of housing during the campaign is treated in Chapter VII.

40. Dewey, Acceptance Speech, *New York Times,* June 25, 1948.

41. Taft to Jesse Barrett, July 12, 1948, Jesse W. Barrett Papers.

42. *Congressional Record,* 80th Cong., 2nd Sess., June 18, 1948, 8734, June 19, 1948, 9321.

43. Truman, "Press Release on the Signing of S. 9790," July 1, 1948, Truman Papers, OF 63.

44. *Ibid.*

45. Unsigned typed White House memorandum, "Should the President Call Congress Back?" June 29, 1948, Rosenman Papers. White House aide David D. Lloyd said that Murphy led the movement among Truman's advisers for the calling of the special session. (Interview with Lloyd, July 21, 1961.) Murphy confirmed Lloyd's statement in an interview on July 26, 1961. For the best analysis of the special session and its political implications, see R. Alton Lee, "The Turnip Session of the Do-Nothing Congress: Presidential Campaign Strategy," *Southwestern Social Science Quarterly,* XLIV (December, 1963), 256-67.

46. Memorandum, "Should the President Call Congress Back?" Rosenman Papers.

47. Congressman Edwin Johnson (Dem., Colo.), in *New York Times,* June 20, 1948; Catholic Trade Union Convention resolution, *New York Times,* July 6, 1948; statements by various congressmen, *New York Times,* June 22, 23, and 29, 1948.

48. Taft, quoted in *New York Times,* June 27, 1948.

49. Truman to Congressman Frank M. Karsten, July 2, 1948, Truman Papers, OF 63-misc.

50. Truman, *Years of Trial and Hope,* 206.

51. Abels, *Out of the Jaws of Victory,* 95-96.

52. Truman, Acceptance Speech, in C. Edgar Brown, ed., *Democracy At Work,* 300-306.

CHAPTER VII

1. *Washington Post,* November 4, 1948, clipping in Vertical File, Harry S Truman Papers; Jules Abels, *Out of the Jaws of Victory,* 249-52.
2. Harry S Truman, *Memoirs,* Vol. II, *Years of Trial and Hope,* 177.
3. Samuel Lubell, *The Future of American Politics, passim;* Abels, *Out of the Jaws of Victory,* 165.
4. Truman, *Years of Trial and Hope,* 171.
5. Truman, Speech at Buffalo, New York, October 8, 1948, Election folders, Charles S. Murphy Files.
6. Speech at Dayton, Ohio, October 11, 1948, Election folders, Murphy Files.
7. Speech at Akron, Ohio, October 11, 1948, Election folders, Murphy Files.
8. Quoted in *Hamilton* (Ohio) *Journal-News,* October 12, 1948.
9. Speech at Evansville, Indiana, September 30, 1948, Election folders, Murphy Files.
10. Speech at New York City, October 28, 1948, Election folders, Murphy Files.
11. Truman, *Years of Trial and Hope,* 211.
12. Text of Taft's statement, *New York Times,* August 10, 1948.
13. Speech at Ashland, Kentucky, October 1, 1948, Election folders, Murphy Files.
14. Truman believed that, because the President is the only public official elected by all Americans, he represents the entire nation—"the people." He developed this idea in a speech at Jefferson City, Missouri, on June 17, 1948, on his "nonpolitical" trip. Norman Podhoretz, in a perceptive essay, discusses Truman's conception of the Presidency and its relationship to the common man. Podhoretz says that Truman, as President, stopped trying to please everyone and created an abstract idea called "the people" with which he identified himself and his political theory. "He identified himself so completely with the people that he was unable to distinguish between his feelings, his needs, and theirs. To please the people was to please himself, for he was the people, he was good old give 'em hell Harry Truman, the ex-haberdasher, 'plain folks' in the White House." Podhoretz, "Truman and the Idea of the Common Man," *Commentary,* XXI (May, 1956), 469-74.
15. Acceptance Speech, in C. Edgar Brown, ed., *Democracy at Work,* 303.
16. Truman, "Message to the Special Session of the Eightieth Congress," July 27, 1948, Truman Papers, OF 63.
17. Truman, *Years of Trial and Hope,* 208.
18. *New York Times,* July 27, 1948.

19. Text of statement by the Republican congressional leadership, *New York Times*, July 28, 1948.

20. *New York Times*, July 29, 1948.

21. *Ibid.*, August 6, 1948.

22. U.S., *Congressional Record*, 80th Cong., 2nd Sess., August 5, 1948, 9869-70.

23. *Ibid.*, 9857-62.

24. *Ibid.*, 9868-69.

25. *Ibid.*, 9868-74.

26. *Ibid.*, 9856.

27. *Ibid.*, August 6, 1948, 9926.

28. *Ibid.*, 9931.

29. *Ibid.*, 9934.

30. *Ibid.*, 9935.

31. *Ibid.*, August 7, 1948, 10207, 10219-20.

32. Truman, "Statement on the Signing of the Housing Bill of 1948," Truman Papers, OF 63.

33. Typed copy, "Summary of action on the President's Recommendations to the Special Session," undated, Special Session folder, Murphy Files.

34. R. Alton Lee, "The Turnip Session of the Do-Nothing Congress: Presidential Campaign Strategy," *Southwestern Social Science Quarterly*, XLIV (December, 1963), 266-67.

35. *Hamilton* (Ohio) *Journal-News*, October 12, 1948.

36. Speech at Buffalo, October 8, 1948, Election folders, Murphy Files.

37. Speech at Madison, Wisconsin, October 14, 1948, Election folders, Murphy Files.

38. Speech at Yonkers, New York, October 29, 1948, Election folders, Murphy Files.

39. Speech at Madison, Wisconsin, October 14, 1948, Election folders, Murphy Files.

40. Speech at Lansing, Michigan, September 6, 1948, Election folders, Murphy Files.

41. Speech at Cincinnati, October 11, 1948, Election folders, Murphy Files.

42. Speech at Wilmington, Delaware, October 29, 1948, Election folders, Murphy Files.

43. Speeches at Buffalo, New York, October 8, 1948; Dayton, Ohio, October 11, 1948; and Pittsburgh, Pennsylvania, October 28, 1948, Election folders, Murphy Files.

44. Speech at New Haven, Connecticut, October 28, 1948, Election folders, Murphy Files.

45. *Ibid.*

46. Speech at Cincinnati, October 11, 1948, Election folders, Murphy Files.

47. Abels, *Out of the Jaws of Victory*, 150.
48. Text of Speech, *New York Times*, October 9, 1948.
49. Abels, *Out of the Jaws of Victory*, 263.
50. Speeches at Buffalo, New York, October 8, 1948; Dayton, Ohio, October 11, 1948; Yonkers, New York, October 29, 1948, Election folders, Murphy Files.
51. Abels, *Out of the Jaws of Victory*, 243.
52. Lubell, *Future of American Politics*, 34.
53. Abels, *Out of the Jaws of Victory*, 269.

CHAPTER VIII

1. Harry S Truman, Speech to the Jefferson-Jackson Dinner, Washington, D.C., February 24, 1949, text of speech in *New York Times*, February 25, 1949.
2. State of the Union Message to Congress, January 5, 1949, Harry S Truman Papers, OF 419-F.
3. David B. Truman, *The Congressional Party*, 145-92.
4. Richard E. Neustadt, "Congress and the Fair Deal; a Legislative Balance Sheet," *Public Policy*, V (1954), 367. Congress expanded social security, increased the minimum wage, established the National Science Foundation, extended soil conservation, and expanded the Rural Electrification Administration, the reclamation, the public power, and the flood control programs.
5. *Ibid.*; William F. Zornow, *America at Mid-Century: the Truman Administration, a Chronicle of Yesterday*, 115.
6. Raymond M. Foley, mimeograph copy of "Statement by Raymond M. Foley, Housing and Home Finance Administrator, before Senate Committee on Banking and Currency on S. 138 and S. 712," February 3, 1949, Truman Papers, OF 63; Marjorie Foulkrod, "Case History of Housing," *Current History*, XV (September, 1948), 138.
7. *Ibid.*; statement by Senator Ralph Flanders, *New York Times*, April 19, 1949.
8. Statement by Raymond M. Foley, *New York Times*, February 4, 1949.
9. Press release, November 10, 1948, Truman Papers, OF 63.
10. State of the Union Message, January 5, 1949, Truman Papers, OF 419-F.
11. U.S., *Congressional Record*, 81st Cong., 1st Sess., January 5, 1949, 48-55.
12. *New York Times*, January 7, 1949; Edith Gunnison Youngblood, "The Position of Robert A. Taft on the Housing Issue," unpublished Master's thesis, University of Connecticut, 48-51.
13. *New York Times*, January 7, 1949; Robert A. Taft, Speech before the Mortgage Bankers Association of America, reported in *The New York Times*, January 26, 1949.

14. *Congressional Record*, 81st Cong., 1st Sess., January 27, 1949, 562.

15. *New York Times*, January 10, 1949.

16. *Ibid.*, January 27, 1949.

17. U.S., Congress, Senate, Committee on Banking and Currency, *Report to Accompany S. 1070*, 81st Cong., 1st Sess., 1949, 15.

18. *New York Times*, February 26, 1949.

19. State of the Union Message, January 5, 1949, Truman Papers, OF 419-F.

20. Tighe Woods, housing expediter, to Roger W. Jones, assistant director of Legislative Reference, Bureau of the Budget, March 30, 1949, Rent Control File, David D. Lloyd Papers.

21. "Statement on the Signing of the Rent Act of 1949," March 30, 1949, Truman Papers, OF 63.

22. *Congressional Record*, 81st Cong., 1st Sess., April 19, 1949, 4730.

23. *New York Times*, April 20, 1949; *Congressional Record*, 81st Cong., 1st Sess., April 19, 1949, 4729.

24. *New York Herald-Tribune*, April 21, 1949, quoted in Youngblood, "The Position of Robert A. Taft on the Housing Issue," 11.

25. *Congressional Record*, 81st Cong., 1st Sess., February 25, 1949, 1552, and January 31, 1949, 713. Senators Cain and Bricker introduced their own housing bill on February 1, 1949; their bill called for government aid to local "mutual associations" on a fifty-fifty basis. This aid would assist the construction of inexpensive housing for low-income groups. Their plan did not entail any further subsidy, whereas the Administration bill called for subsidy for forty years. The Bricker-Cain bill was not reported by the Senate Banking and Currency Committee. See Harry P. Cain to Senator Tom Connally, February 9, 1949, Thomas C. Connally Papers.

26. *Congressional Record*, 81st Cong., 1st Sess., April 21, 1949, 4849.

27. *Ibid.*, April 20, 1949, 4802.

28. *Ibid.*, April 21, 1949, 4850.

29. *Ibid.*, 4852.

30. *Ibid.*, 4855.

31. *Ibid.*, 4860.

32. *Ibid.*, 4903.

33. *Ibid.*, April 4, 1949, 3830.

34. U.S., Congress, House, Committee on Banking and Currency, *Report to Accompany S. 1070*, 81st Cong., 1st Sess., May 16, 1949.

35. *New York Times*, May 18, 1949.

36. *Ibid.*, May 25, 26, and 27, 1949.

37. *Ibid.*, June 8, 1949.

38. David B. Truman, *The Congressional Party*, 18; *New York Times*, June 8, 1949.

39. *New York Times*, June 15, 1949.

40. *Headlines*, XVI (June 20, 1949).

41. *New York Times*, July 1, 1949.

42. *Ibid.*, June 19, 1949.

43. Press release of Harry S Truman to Sam Rayburn, June 17, 1949, Truman Papers, OF 63.

44. *New York Times*, June 23, 1949. A detailed typewritten account of the altercation is in the Raymond M. Foley Papers.

45. *Congressional Record*, 81st Cong., 1st Sess., June 22, 1949, 8131-33.

46. Picture in *New York Times*, June 23, 1949.

47. *Congressional Record*, 81st Cong., 1st Sess., June 29, 1949, 8636, 8667-68.

48. *Ibid.*, 8677-78.

49. *Congressional Quarterly Almanac*, V (1949), 284.

50. Taft to Truman, July 14, 1949, Taft Folder, Truman Papers, PPF.

51. Tobey to Truman, July 16, 1949, Truman Papers, OF 63.

52. Lee Johnson, executive vice-president of the National Public Housing Conference, to Truman, July 12, 1949, William O'Dwyer, president of the United States Conference of Mayors, to Truman, July 7, 1949, Philip Murray, president of the CIO, to Truman, July 7, 1949, Truman Papers, OF 63.

53. Truman to Tobey, July 20, 1949, Truman Papers, OF 63.

54. Typed list, "Those to be present at signing of Housing Bill of 1949," Truman Papers, OF 63. Those present were: Secretary of Agriculture Charles F. Brannan; Congressmen Burnet Maybank, John J. Sparkman, Ralph Flanders, Brent Spence, Wright Patman, M. H. Mike Monroney; Raymond M. Foley; John T. Egan, commissioner of the Public Housing Administration; B. T. Fitzpatrick, counsel for the Housing and Home Finance Agency; David Lawrence, vice-president of the United States Conference of Mayors; John T. Taylor of the American Legion; Jack Carter, national housing officer of the Veterans of Foreign Wars; Francis Sullivan, national legislative director of the Disabled Veterans; Harold Keats, national commander of the AMVETS; James Carey, secretary-treasurer of the CIO; William Green, president of the AFL; Lee Johnson, executive vice-president of the National Public Housing Conference; Larry Cox, president of the National Association of Housing Officials; A. E. Lyons, executive secretary of the Railway Labor Executive Association; Jeanetta Welch Brown, executive director of the National Council of Negro Women; and Harry Lee, national legislative representative of the Brotherhood of Railroad Trainmen.

55. Truman, "Statement on the Signing of the National Housing Act of 1949," July 15, 1949, Truman Papers, OF 63.
56. Neustadt, *op. cit.*, 367; Louis W. Koenig, "Truman's Global Leadership," *Current History*, XXXIX (October, 1960), 229; Zornow, *America at Mid-Century*, 115.
57. A congressional district is termed "urban" if it contained, in 1950, a standard metropolitan district within its borders.
58. *Congressional Record*, 81st Cong., 1st Sess., June 22, 1949, 8131.
59. U.S., Congress, *Conference Report to Accompany S. 1070*, 81st Cong., 1st Sess., July 6, 1949, 1.
60. Truman to W. D. Morison, president of the National Association of Real Estate Brokers, August 22, 1949, Truman Papers, PPF 5822.

CHAPTER IX

1. Harry Conn, "Housing: A Vanishing Vision," *New Republic*, CXXV (August 13, 1951), 15-16.
2. *Historical Statistics of the United States, Colonial Times to 1957*, 393.
3. The terms "upper," "lower," and "middle" income groups are, of course, abstract. They are used here because this was the terminology used by the supporters of the bill. Even Raymond M. Foley, Housing and Home Finance administrator, could not adequately and precisely define the group termed as "middle income families." Testimony of Foley, U.S., Congress, Senate, Committee on Banking and Currency, *Hearings on S. 2246*, 81st Cong., 2nd Sess., January 12, 1950, 12-13.
4. Harry S Truman to Murray D. Lincoln, toastmaster of the Middle Income Housing Conference Dinner, February 21, 1950, Harry S Truman Papers, PPF 1491.
5. Testimony of Foley, Senate, Committee on Banking and Currency, *Hearings on S. 2246*, January 12, 1950, 13-14; Truman, Economic Report to Congress, January 6, 1950, 16, typed report, "Middle Income Housing Program," by the Housing and Home Finance Agency, December 17, 1949, 6, David D. Lloyd Files, Truman Papers.
6. U.S., *Congressional Record*, 81st Cong., 1st Sess., June 12, 1949, 9288.
7. Walter Reuther, CIO housing chairman; Edward Weinfeld, president of the National Housing Conference; William Green, president of AFL; and Msgr. John O'Grady, secretary of the National Conference of Catholic Charities, to Truman, August 11, 1949, Truman Papers, OF 63; Donald and Astrid Monson, "Ideas from Sweden," *American City*, LXIV (March, 1949), 84-86; (April,

1949), 110-11; (May, 1949), 140-42; Catharine Bauer, "The Middle Class Needs Housing Too," *New Republic*, CXXI (August 29, 1949), 17-20.

8. Truman, memorandum to Brent Spence, chairman of the House Banking and Currency Committee, March 20, 1950, Truman Papers, OF 63.

9. Truman, State of the Union Message, January 4, 1950, Truman Papers, OF 419-F.

10. Testimony of Rodney M. Lockwood, president of the National Association of Home Builders, Senate, Committee on Banking and Currency, *Hearings on S. 2246*, January 17, 1950, 194-214; testimony of John C. Thompson, representative of the National Association of Real Estate Boards, *ibid.*, January 13, 1950, 112-13.

11. Testimony of Horace Russell, representative of United States Savings and Loan League, *ibid.*, 107.

12. *Ibid.*, 101-11.

13. *New York Times*, February 24, 1950.

14. For example, the American Institute of Architects, which had supported public housing, asked, "Is the measure necessary?" in a letter to the Senate Banking and Currency Committee, printed in Senate, Committee on Banking and Currency, *Hearings on S. 2246*, 283; *New York Times*, February 16, March 23 and 27, 1950; Walter Reuther to Truman, March 20, 1950, Lloyd Files, Truman Papers.

15. *Congressional Record*, 81st Cong., 2nd Sess., March 14, 1950, 3272-82, March 15, 1950, 3355-57.

16. The following veterans' groups announced their endorsement of the bill: American Veterans' Committee, Catholic War Veterans, Jewish War Veterans, American Legion, Veterans of Foreign Wars, and the AMVETS.

17. *Congressional Record*, 81st Cong., 2nd Sess., May 15, 1950, 3385; David D. Lloyd to Charles S. Murphy, typed memorandum, "Regarding the Defeat of Title III," March 16, 1950, Lloyd Files, Truman Papers.

18. The following Democrats opposed the bill: John Stennis (Miss.), Walter George and Richard Russell (Ga.), Willis Robertson and Harry Byrd (Va.), Allen J. Ellender (La.), John McClellan and William Fulbright (Ark.), Clyde Hoey (N.C.), Spessard Holland (Fla.), Guy Gillette (Iowa), and Millard Tydings and Herbert O'Conor (Md.). Only Robertson and McClellan had voted against the Housing Act of 1949, and only McClellan, Hoey, Holland, and Olin Johnston (S.C.) had voted against an amendment to remove public housing from the Housing Act of 1949. Also, Republican bipartisan support, widely evident in 1949, melted away in 1950. Robert Taft and Charles Tobey, for example, did not appear on the floor to vote on the Housing Act of 1950.

19. Almost no public opinion mail arrived at the White House,

although large quantities of it arrived throughout the four years prior to the passage of the Housing Act of 1949.

20. Truman, memorandum to Brent Spence, March 20, 1950, Truman Papers, OF 63.

21. *Congressional Record*, 81st Cong., 2nd Sess., March 22, 1950, 3881-82; Truman to William Green, president of the AFL, March 27, 1950, Truman Papers, OF 63.

22. *Congressional Record*, 81st Cong., 2nd Sess., April 6, 1950, 4919.

23. *New York Times*, April 21, 1950.

24. State of the Union Message, January 4, 1950, Truman Papers, OF 419-F. Truman probably based his decision on a typed memorandum, "Basic Considerations on the Extension of Rent Control," January 2, 1950, Truman Papers, OF 63-A. The memorandum was unsigned, but most likely was written by Housing Expediter Tighe Woods. The memorandum said, in part, "The bulk of the nation's rental housing is in the metropolitan areas which have the most acute housing shortages and exercise a definite influence on the national economy. The need in these areas alone justifies the extension of Federal rent control until June, 1951." The memorandum also stated that the end of controls could probably be achieved at that time because of the high rate of housing construction, which "should bring supply closer in balance with demand."

25. Truman, press release of Message to Congress, April 21, 1950, Truman Papers, OF 63-A; see also Chester Bowles, governor of Connecticut, to Truman, April 14, 1950, Truman Papers, OF 63-A. Bowles told Truman that rents in many areas of the nation would rise up to 40 per cent if controls were ended.

26. A large quantity of public opinion mail in Truman Papers (O-355, O-556, and 63-A misc.) reflects great interest by both parties. Most of the mail is from landlords.

27. John McCormack, memorandum to Matt Connelly, White House aide, April 1, 1950, Truman Papers, OF 63-A.

28. *Congressional Record*, 81st Cong., 2nd Sess., June 12, 1950, 8427, 8455.

29. *Ibid.*, June 7, 1950, 8224-42, June 9, 1950, 8355-57, and June 12, 1950, 8420.

30. *Ibid.*, June 13, 1950, 8553.

31. Tighe Woods to John Steelman, June 20, 1950, Truman Papers, OF 63.

32. *New York Times*, November 28 and 30, 1950. Truman wrote to Maybank, "There has been a marked change in the situation since the law was passed. . . . To carry this program [the Korean War] successfully and to safeguard our economy, it will be necessary to keep rents in vital defense areas from rising to unreasonable levels."

33. *Congressional Record*, 81st Cong., 2nd Sess., December 7, 1950, 16253, 16306.

34. Paul Wendt, *Housing Policy—the Search for Solutions*, 155-57; press release, June 31, 1951, Truman Papers, OF 63-A. On July 31, 1951, the Office of Housing Expediter was terminated.

35. *To Secure These Rights, the Report of the President's Committee on Civil Rights.*

36. Typed, unsigned memorandum, "The Housing Bill of 1949 and the struggle over Segregation," July 7, 1949, Clark Clifford Files, Truman Papers; David K. Niles, White House aide, memorandum to Truman, October 21, 1949, Truman, memorandum to Carl R. Gray, administrator of Veterans' Affairs, November 1, 1949, Truman Papers, OF 63; Charles Abrams, "Human Rights in Slum Clearance," *Survey*, LXXXVI (January, 1950), 27-28; Charles Abrams, *Forbidden Neighbors*, 229; Housing and Home Finance Agency, *Housing of the Non-white Population 1940-1950*, 3.

37. *Fifth Annual Report*, Housing and Home Finance Agency, 1952, 413.

38. Charles Abrams, "The Segregation Threat in Housing," in Nathan Straus, *Two-Thirds of a Nation; A Housing Program*, 219-23.

39. "Equality in Housing," *New Republic*, CXXI (December 19, 1949), 8.

40. Abrams, "The Segregation Threat in Housing," *op. cit.*, 222; Eunice and George Grier, *Privately Developed Interracial Housing*, 21.

41. Abrams, "The Segregation Threat in Housing," *op. cit.*, 222; Hortense W. Gabel, director of the National Committee Against Discrimination in Housing, to Raymond M. Foley, February 26, 1953, Foley Papers. *The San Francisco Sun Reporter* (Negro newspaper), June 28, 1952, stated, "We think Mr. Foley is attempting to give bone and sinew to the President's strong declaration for Civil Rights." Clipping in Truman Papers, OF 63; *New York Times*, January 22, 1951.

42. *Sixth Annual Report*, Housing and Home Finance Agency, 1952, 405.

43. *Ibid.*, 402-4, 57, 60; Jack H. Bryan, director of information for the HHFA, typed copy, "Brief Summary of the Housing Act of 1949," Truman Papers, OF 1282.

44. Straus, *Two-Thirds of a Nation*, 118-19, 256-58, 275-81.

45. *Sixth Annual Report*, Housing and Home Finance Agency, 1952, 406; *New York Times*, October 18, 1950.

46. Jean Bergman, "Real Estate Lobby Side Show," *New Republic*, CXXII (March 20, 1950), 10-11; Harry Conn, "Housing: A Vanishing Vision," *New Republic*, CXXV (July 30, 1951), 12-13; "Public Housing Gets a Drubbing," *Business Week*, May 27, 1950, 26; Martin Meyerson and Edward C. Banfield, *Politics, Planning*

and the Public Interest; The Case of Public Housing in Chicago, 117-18.

47. *New York Times,* February 26, 1950; *American City,* LXVI (January, 1951), 7; Conn, *op. cit.* (July 23, 1951), 10, and (July 30, 1951), 12-13; Lee F. Johnson, "Housing: A 1950 Tragedy," *Survey,* LXXXVI (December, 1950), 551-55; Bergman, *op. cit.*

48. Conn, *op. cit.* (July 23, 1951), 10.

49. Conn, *op. cit.* (August 13, 1951), 15; Karl Schriftgiesser, *The Lobbyists,* 216-23.

50. Conn, *op. cit.* (July 23, 1951), 15-16.

51. Lee Johnson to Truman, December 18, 1950, Truman Papers, OF 63.

52. *Ibid.;* Bauer, "The Middle Class Needs Housing Too," *op. cit.;* Robert S. Allen and William V. Shannon, *The Truman Merry-Go-Round,* 39.

53. Foley, Speech before the National Association of Home Builders, Dallas, Texas, October 24, 1947, Foley Papers.

54. Foley, radio address over the Arrowhead Radio Network of Minnesota, March 3, 1950, Foley Papers; Foley's statement before the Senate Banking and Currency Committee on the Reorganization Plan No. 3, June 18, 1947, and Speech to the National Public Housing Conference, March 12, 1947, Foley Papers.

55. Bauer, "The Middle Class Needs Housing Too," *op. cit.,* 18; Oscar Kreutz, executive manager of the National Savings and Loan League, to Foley, February 27, 1953, Foley Papers; *Business Week,* September 10, 1949, 6.

56. Foley, Speech before the National Association of Housing Officials, October 13, 1948, Foley Papers.

57. *New York Times,* April 4, 1950.

58. Lee Johnson to Truman, December 18, 1950, Truman Papers, OF 63; Ira Robbins, chairman of the Board of the National Public Housing Conference, to Truman, February 20, 1952, Truman Papers, OF 63-misc.

59. David D. Lloyd and Richard E. Neustadt, memorandum to Charles S. Murphy, November 18, 1950, Lloyd Files, Truman Papers.

60. *New York Times,* July 19, 1950; Meyerson and Banfield, *op. cit.,* 23; Samuel E. Trotter, "A Study of Public Housing in the United States," unpublished doctoral dissertation, University of Alabama, 208.

61. Msgr. John O'Grady and others to Truman, August 4, 1950, John Steelman to Truman, August 22, 1950, Truman Papers, OF 63; Foley, Speech over WMAL Radio (Washington, D.C.), December 4, 1950, Foley Papers.

62. *New York Times,* October 18, 1950; John Steelman to Congressman Raymond Karst, November 7, 1950, Truman Papers, OF 151.

63. *New York Times,* October 18, 1950.

64. *Historical Statistics of the United States, Colonial Times to 1957,* 393; *Newsweek,* XXVI (September 10, 1951), 80.

65. Truman to Vincent Impellitteri, mayor of New York, May 31, 1951, Truman Papers, OF 63; *New York Times,* December 27, 1950, and March 20, 1951; Jack H. Bryan, director of information of the Housing and Home Finance Agency, to Mrs. Cook (no first name given) of Pueblo, Colorado, November 21, 1950, Housing and Home Finance Agency Papers; Truman to Burnet Maybank, May 22, 1951, Truman Papers, OF 63.

66. *Fifth Annual Report,* Housing and Home Finance Agency, 1951, 53-54.

67. *Ibid.,* 391-95.

68. *Congressional Record,* 82nd Cong., 1st Sess., May 5, 1951, 4897, 4899-4900; Foley to Charles S. Murphy, May 8, 1951, Truman Papers, OF 63.

69. Truman to Maybank, May 22, 1951, Truman Papers, OF 63.

70. *Congressional Record,* 82nd Cong., 1st Sess., June 20, 1951, 6795, July 25, 1951, 8875; *Congressional Record,* 82nd Cong., 2nd Sess., March 20, 1952, 2627, June 3, 1952, 6461.

CHAPTER X

1. Samuel Lubell, *The Future of American Politics,* 8-28.

2. Staughton Lynd, "Urban Renewal—For Whom?" *Commentary,* XXXI (January, 1961), 40. In 1961, Congress passed the Kennedy Administration's "Omnibus Housing Bill," which provided for the building of 100,000 units of public housing. Only token opposition arose against this provision; obviously, the real estate lobby believed that public housing posed little or no threat to the housing industry.

3. Paul F. Wendt, *Housing Policy—the Search for Solutions,* 190-96; Jane Jacobs, *The Death and Life of Great American Cities, passim;* Roy Lubove, *The Progressives and the Slums; Tenement House Reform in New York, 1890-1917,* 245-56; Harrison Salisbury, *The Shook-Up Generation,* 61-73; Lynd, *op. cit.,* 34-46; Daniel Seligman, "The Enduring Slums," *Fortune,* LVI (December, 1957), 214, 221; Morton S. Baratz, "Public Housing: A Critique and a Proposal," *Social Research,* XX (October, 1953), 332-44; Michael Harrington, "Slums, Old and New," *Commentary,* XXX (August, 1960), 118-19; H. Warren Dunham and Nathan D. Grundstein, "The Impact of a Confusion of Social Objectives on Public Housing: A Preliminary Analysis," *Marriage and Family Living,* XXII (May, 1955), 103-12; Catharine Bauer, "Housing, Planning and Public Policy," *ibid.,* 101-2; Catharine Bauer, "The Dreary Deadlock of Public Housing," *Architectural Forum,* CVI (May, 1957), 140 ff.;

"The Dreary Deadlock of Public Housing and How to Break It," *Architectural Forum,* CVI (June, 1957), 139 ff.; editorial, *Recreation,* LIII (November, 1960), 404.

4. Louis S. Katz, director, Statistics Branch, Public Housing Administration, to me, August 27, 1964.

5. Editors of *Fortune, The Exploding Metropolis,* 92.

6. Seligman, *op. cit.,* 144 ff.

7. For example, see Bauer, "The Dreary Deadlock of Public Housing," *passim;* Baratz, *op. cit., passim;* Elisabeth Wood, quoted in *Architectural Forum,* CXV (September, 1961), 8-9; Wendt, *op. cit.,* 190-96, 217-25.

8. Jacobs, *op. cit.,* 4.

9. Salisbury, *op. cit.,* 62.

10. *Ibid.,* 63.

11. Lubove, *op. cit.,* 255-56.

12. Bauer, "The Dreary Deadlock of Public Housing," *op. cit.,* 140 ff.

13. Wendt, *op. cit.,* 217-25; Seligman, *op. cit., passim;* Dunham and Grundstein, *op. cit.,* 103-12; Lynd, *op. cit.,* 34-46.

14. Bauer, "The Dreary Deadlock of Public Housing," *op. cit.,* 141.

15. See Table VI-14, "Why Families Move From Low-Rent Housing," in Wendt, *op. cit.,* 195; see also 190-96.

16. Lynd, *op. cit.,* 34-44; Bauer, "The Dreary Deadlock of Public Housing," *op. cit.,* 141; Harrington, *op. cit.,* 118-24.

17. Salisbury, *op. cit.,* 61-73.

18. Eric Goldman, *Rendezvous With Destiny,* 155-57, 213-19, 337-47.

19. *Sixteenth Annual Report,* Housing and Home Finance Agency, 1962, 283.

20. Bauer, "The Dreary Deadlock of Public Housing," *op. cit.,* 140.

Bibliography

A. MANUSCRIPTS

Wat Arnold Papers. Western Historical Manuscripts Collection, University of Missouri, Columbia.

Jesse W. Barrett Papers. Western Historical Manuscripts Collection, University of Missouri, Columbia.

Clark Clifford Papers. Harry S Truman Library, Independence, Missouri.

William C. Cole Papers. Western Historical Manuscripts Collection, University of Missouri, Columbia.

Thomas C. Connally Papers. Library of Congress, Washington, D.C.

Democratic National Committee Papers. Harry S Truman Library, Independence, Missouri.

Raymond M. Foley Papers. Harry S Truman Library, Independence, Missouri.

Office of Housing Expediter Papers. National Archives, Washington, D.C.

Housing and Home Finance Agency Papers. Housing and Home Finance Agency, Washington, D.C.

David D. Lloyd Papers. Harry S Truman Library, Independence, Missouri.

J. Howard McGrath Papers. Harry S Truman Library, Independence, Missouri.

Charles S. Murphy Files. Harry S Truman Library, Independence, Missouri.

Records of the White House Reporter. Harry S Truman Library, Independence, Missouri.

Samuel I. Rosenman Papers. Harry S Truman Library, Independence, Missouri.

Harry S Truman Papers. Harry S Truman Library, Independence, Missouri.

Robert F. Wagner Papers. Georgetown University, Washington, D.C.

James Webb Papers. Harry S Truman Library, Independence, Missouri.

B. GOVERNMENT DOCUMENTS

All of the following documents were published at various dates by the Government Printing Office in Washington, D.C.

Housing and Home Finance Agency. *Fifth Annual Report,* 1951; *Sixth Annual Report,* 1952; *Sixteenth Annual Report,* 1962.

National Resources Planning Board. *Report.* 1943.

U.S. Congress. *Conference Report to Accompany S. 1070.* 81st Cong., 1st Sess., 1949.

———, Joint Committee on Housing. *Final Majority Report.* March 15, 1948.

U.S. *Congressional Record.* 77th Cong., 2nd Sess., through 82nd Cong., 2nd Sess., 1942-52.

U.S. House of Representatives, Committee on Banking and Currency. *Hearings on Housing Act of 1949.* 81st Cong., 1st Sess., April 7 and May 9, 1949. *Report to Accompany S. 1070.* 81st Cong., 1st Sess., 1949.

———, Special Committee on Lobbying Activities. *Hearings.* 81st Cong., 2nd Sess., 1950.

U.S. Senate, Committee on Banking and Currency. *Hearings on S. 2246.* 81st Cong., 2nd Sess., January 12-18 and February 16, 1950. *Report to Accompany S. 1952.* 79th Cong., 2nd Sess., 1952. *Report to Accompany S. 866.* 80th Cong., 1st Sess., 1947. *Report to Accompany S. 1070.* 81st Cong., 1st Sess., 1949.

———, Committee on Rules, Subcommittee on Privileges and Elections. *Report.* 82nd Cong., 2nd Sess., 1952.

———, Special Committee on Postwar Economic Policy and Planning, Subcommittee on Housing and Urban Redevelopment. *Hearings Pursuant to S. Res. 102* (78th Cong.). January 6, 1945-February 7, 1945. *Report.* 79th Cong., 1st Sess., 1945.

C. GOVERNMENT PUBLICATIONS

All of the following publications were published at various dates by the Government Printing Office in Washington, D.C.

Ellender, Allen J., "Objections to the Wagner-Ellender-Taft Bill (S. 1592) Are Not Valid." 1946.
Flanders, Ralph E., "High Cost of Housing, Report to Joint Committee on Housing." 1948.
Gamble, Ralph, "Statistics on Housing, Final Majority Report of the Joint Committee on Housing." 1948.
Housing and Home Finance Agency, "For the Home-Buying Veteran." 1949.
——, "Housing Activities of the Federal Government." 1952.
——, "Housing of the Non-white Population, 1940-1950." 1952.
——, "The 1950 Housing Situation in Charts." 1950.
——, "Slum Clearance and Urban Redevelopment." 1950.
——, "Summary of the Evolution of Housing Activities in the Federal Government." 1950.
McCarthy, Joseph R., "Report to the Joint Committee on Housing." 1948.
——, "Individual Views." 1948.
"Toward Unity in Postwar Housing." 1945.

D. NEWSPAPERS

The New York Times. January 1, 1943-February 1, 1953.
Hamilton (Ohio) *Journal-News.* October 12, 1948.

E. INTERVIEWS

Raymond M. Foley, July 25, 1961, Washington, D.C.
David D. Lloyd, July 20, 1961, Washington, D.C.
Charles S. Murphy, July 26, 1961, Washington, D.C.
Harry S Truman, July 11, 1961, Independence, Missouri.

F. UNPUBLISHED STUDIES

Bredemeier, Harry C., "The Federal Public Housing Movement." Doctoral dissertation, Columbia University, 1955.
Parker, Daniel P., "Political and Social Views of Harry S. Truman." Doctoral dissertation, University of Pennsylvania, 1951.
Rogge, Edward A., "The Speech-making of Harry S. Truman." Doctoral dissertation, University of Missouri, 1958.
Schmidtlein, Eugene F., "Truman the Senator." Doctoral dissertation, University of Missouri, 1962.
Trotter, Samuel E., "A Study of Public Housing in the United States." Doctoral dissertation, University of Alabama, 1956.
Youngblood, Ethel Gunnison, "The Position of Robert A. Taft on the Housing Issue." Master's thesis, University of Connecticut, 1957.

G. BOOKS

Abels, Jules, *Out of the Jaws of Victory.* New York: Henry Holt & Company, Inc., 1959.

Abrams, Charles, *Forbidden Neighbors.* New York: Harper and Brothers, 1955.

———, *The Future of Housing.* New York: Harper and Brothers, 1946.

Agar, Herbert, *The Price of Power.* Chicago: The University of Chicago Press, 1957.

Allen, George E., *Presidents Who Have Known Me.* New York: Simon & Schuster, Inc., 1950.

Allen, Robert S., and Shannon, William V., *The Truman Merry-Go-Round.* New York: The Vanguard Press, 1950.

Atherton, Lewis E., *Main Street on the Middle Border.* Bloomington: Indiana University Press, 1954.

Banfield, Edward, *Government and Housing in Metropolitan Areas.* New York: McGraw-Hill Book Company, Inc., 1958.

Beyer, Glenn H., *Housing: A Factual Analysis.* New York: The Macmillan Company, 1958.

Braeman, John, Bremner, Robert H., and Walters, Everett, eds., *Change and Continuity in Twentieth-Century America.* Columbus: Ohio State University Press, 1964.

Bremner, Robert, *From the Depths.* New York: New York University Press, 1956.

Brown, C. Edgar, ed., *Democracy at Work.* Philadelphia: Local Democratic Committee of Pennsylvania, 1948.

Brown, Robert K., *Public Housing in Action; The Record of Pittsburgh.* Pittsburgh: University of Pittsburgh Press, 1959.

Chambers, Clarke A., *Seedtime of Reform: American Social Service and Social Action, 1918-1933.* Minneapolis: The University of Minnesota Press, 1963.

Churchill, Henry S., *The City is the People.* New York: Reynal & Hitchcock, 1945.

Clemens, Cyril, *The Man From Missouri.* Webster Groves, Missouri: International Mark Twain Society, 1945.

Coffin, Tris, *Missouri Compromise.* Boston: Little, Brown & Company, 1947.

Conkin, Paul, *Tomorrow a New World: The New Deal Community Program.* Ithaca: Cornell University Press, 1959.

Connery, Robert H., and Leach, Richard H., *The Federal Government and Metropolitan Areas.* Cambridge: Harvard University Press, 1960.

Current Biography. New York: H. W. Wilson Company, 1941, 1945, 1946, 1949.

Daniels, Jonathan, *The Man of Independence.* Philadelphia: J. B. Lippincott Company, 1950.

Fisher, Robert Moore, *Twenty Years of Public Housing*. New York: Harper and Brothers, 1959.
Flanders, Ralph E., *Senator From Vermont*. Boston: Little, Brown & Company, 1961.
Editors of *Fortune, The Exploding Metropolis*. Garden City: Doubleday & Company, Inc., 1959.
Gallaher, Art, *Plainville Fifteen Years Later*. New York: Columbia University Press, 1961.
Goldman, Eric, *The Crucial Decade and After, America 1945-1960*. New York: Vintage Books, 1960.
——, *Rendezvous With Destiny*. New York: Vintage Books, 1958.
Grantham, Dewey, *The Democratic South*. Athens: The University of Georgia Press, 1963.
Gray, George Herbert, *Housing and Citizenship*. New York: Reinhold Publishing Corporation, 1946.
Grier, Eunice and George, *Privately Developed Interracial Housing*. Berkeley: University of California Press, 1960.
Grimes, Alan P., *Equality in America; Religion, Race and the Urban Majority*. New York: Oxford University Press, 1964.
Heard, Alexander, *A Two-Party South?* Chapel Hill: The University of North Carolina Press, 1952.
Helm, William P., *Harry Truman, A Political Biography*. New York: Duell, Sloan & Pearce, Inc., 1947.
Historical Statistics of the United States, Colonial Times to 1957. Washington: Government Printing Office, 1960.
Hodgins, Eric, *Mr. Blandings Builds His Dream House*. New York: Simon & Schuster, Inc., 1946.
Jacobs, Jane, *The Death and Life of Great American Cities*. New York: Vintage Books, 1963.
Johnson, Walter, *1600 Pennsylvania Avenue*. Boston: Little, Brown & Company, 1960.
Keats, John, *The Crack in the Picture Window*. Boston: Houghton Mifflin Company, 1956.
Key, V. O., *Southern Politics in State and Nation*. New York: Alfred A. Knopf, Inc., 1949.
Lasch, Robert, *Breaking the Building Blockade*. Chicago: The University of Chicago Press, 1946.
Leuchtenburg, William E., *Franklin D. Roosevelt and the New Deal, 1932-1940*. New York: Harper and Brothers, 1963.
Lubell, Samuel, *The Future of American Politics*. New York: Harper and Brothers, 1951.
Lubove, Roy, *The Progressives and the Slums; Tenement House Reform in New York City, 1890-1917*. Pittsburgh: University of Pittsburgh Press, 1962.
——, *Community Planning in the 1920's: The Contribution of the Regional Planning Association of America*. Pittsburgh: University of Pittsburgh Press, 1963.

McDonnell, Timothy, *The Wagner Housing Act*. Chicago: Loyola University Press, 1957.

McGrath, J. Howard, *The Power of the People*. New York: Julian Messner, Inc., 1948.

McNaughton, Frank, and Hehmeyer, Walter, *Harry Truman, President*. New York: McGraw-Hill Book Company, Inc., 1948.

——, *This Man Truman*. New York: McGraw-Hill Book Company, Inc., 1945.

Madison, Charles A., *Leaders and Liberals in 20th Century America*. New York: Frederick Ungar Publishing Co., Inc., 1961.

Martin, Joe, *My First Fifty Years in Politics*. New York: McGraw-Hill Book Company, Inc., 1960.

Mauldin, Bill, *Back Home*. New York: William Sloane Associates, 1947.

Meyerson, Martin, and Banfield, Edward C., *Politics, Planning and the Public Interest; The Case of Public Housing in Chicago*. Glencoe, Illinois: Free Press of Glencoe, Inc., 1955.

Rogg, Nat, *A History of the Veterans' Emergency Housing Program*. Washington: Housing Expediter Office, 1948.

Rosenman, Dorothy, *A Million Homes a Year*. New York: Harcourt, Brace & Company, Inc., 1945.

Rosenman, Samuel I., ed., *The Public Papers and Addresses of Franklin D. Roosevelt*. 1943 Volume, *The Tide Turns*; 1944-45 Volume, *Victory and the Threshold of Peace*. New York, Harper and Brothers, 1950.

——, *Working with Roosevelt*. New York: Harper and Brothers, 1952.

Rovere, Richard H., *Senator Joe McCarthy*. New York: Meridian Books, 1960.

Salisbury, Harrison, *The Shook-Up Generation*. Greenwich, Connecticut: Fawcett Publications, Inc., 1958.

Schauffler, Edward R., *Harry Truman, Son of the Soil*. Kansas City: Schauffler Publishing Company, 1947.

Schriftgiesser, Karl, *The Lobbyists*. Boston: Little, Brown & Company, 1951.

Sindler, Allan P., *Huey Long's Louisiana*. Baltimore: The Johns Hopkins Press, 1956.

Steinberg, Alfred, *The Man From Missouri: The Life and Times of Harry S. Truman*. New York: G. P. Putnam's Sons, 1962.

Straus, Nathan, *The Seven Myths of Housing*. New York: Alfred A. Knopf, Inc., 1944.

——, *Two-Thirds of a Nation; A Housing Program*. New York: Alfred A. Knopf, Inc., 1952.

To Secure These Rights, the Report of the President's Committee on Civil Rights. Washington: Government Printing Office, 1947.

Truman, David B., *The Congressional Party*. New York: John Wiley & Sons, Inc., 1959.

Truman, Harry S, *Memoirs.* Vol. I, *Year of Decisions;* Vol. II, *Years of Trial and Hope.* Garden City: Doubleday & Company, Inc., 1955, 1956.
———, *Public Papers of the Presidents of the United States, Harry S Truman, 1945.* Washington: Government Printing Office, 1961.
———, *Public Papers of the Presidents of the United States, Harry S Truman, 1946.* Washington: Government Printing Office, 1962.
Vidich, Arthur, and Bensman, Joseph, *Small Town in Mass Society; Class, Power and Religion in a Rural Community.* Princeton: Princeton University Press, 1958.
Voorhis, Jerry, *Confessions of a Congressman.* New York: Doubleday & Company, Inc., 1947.
Weaver, Robert C., *The Negro Ghetto.* New York: Harcourt, Brace & Company, Inc., 1948.
Wendt, Paul F., *Housing Policy—the Search for Solutions.* Berkeley: University of California Press, 1963.
———, *The Role of the Federal Government in Housing.* Washington: American Enterprise Association, 1956.
White, William S., *The Taft Story.* New York: Harper and Brothers, 1954.
Zornow, William Frank, *America at Mid-Century: the Truman Administration, a Chronicle of Yesterday.* Cleveland: Howard Allen, Inc., 1959.

H. ARTICLES

Abrams, Charles, "Government and Housing." *Nation,* CLIX (October 21, 1944), 498.
———, "Homeless America." *Nation,* CLXIII (December 21, 1946), 723-25; (December 28, 1946), 753-55; CLXIV (January 4, 1947), 15-16.
———, "Human Rights in Slum Clearance." *Survey,* LXXXVI (January, 1950), 27-28.
———, "A Plank in a Platform." *Nation,* CLXVI (May 15, 1948), 548-51.
———, "The Segregation Threat in Housing." *Commentary,* VII (February, 1949), 123-31.
American City, LVIII (June, 1943), 58; LXVI (January, 1951), 7.
Baratz, Morton S., "Public Housing: A Critique and a Proposal." *Social Research,* XX (October, 1953), 332-44.
Bates, Harry C., "Crisis in Housing." *American Federationist,* LIII (January, 1946), 11-13, 31.
———, "Homes for the Future." *American Federationist,* LI (June, 1944), 9-11.
———, "Housing—For Whom?" *American Federationist,* LIII (December, 1946), 3-7.

——, "Housing Truths." *American Federationist*, LV (August, 1948), 5-7.

——, "Let's Act on Housing." *American Federationist*, LVI (January, 1949), 5.

——, "Two Must Bills." *American Federationist*, LVI (February, 1949), 6-8.

——, "Victory in Housing." *American Federationist*, LVI (July, 1949), 10.

——, "Your New Home—When?" *American Federationist*, LIV (June, 1947), 12-13, 27.

Bauer, Catharine, "The Dreary Deadlock of Public Housing." *Architectural Forum*, CVI (May, 1957), 140-42, 219, 221.

——, "Freedom of Choice." *Nation*, CLXVI (May 15, 1948), 533-37.

——, "Housing, Planning and Public Policy." *Marriage and Family Living*, XVII (May, 1955), 101-2.

——, "The Middle Class Needs Housing Too." *New Republic*, CXXI (August 29, 1949), 17-20.

Bergman, Jean, "Real Estate Lobby Side Show." *New Republic*, CXXII (March 20, 1950), 10-11.

Binsse, Harry, "A Place to Lay Your Head." *Commonweal*, XXXIX (December 31, 1943), 270-73.

Blandford, John B., Jr., "Speech Before the National Association of Housing Officials." *American City*, LVIII (June, 1943), 58.

Business Week, December, 1944, 21-22.

"Canning the Planners." *Commonweal*, XXXVIII (June 11, 1943), 192.

Carr, Edward, "Is Private Enterprise Doing an Adequate Housing Job?" *Vital Speeches*, XIV (May 1, 1948), 438-43.

Chambers, Clarke A., "Creative Effort in an Age of Normalcy, 1918-1933." *The Social Welfare Forum*, 1961, 252-71.

Coffin, Tris, "John R. Steelman." *New Republic*, CXV (November 11, 1946), 625-26.

——, "The Slickest Lobby." *Nation*, CLXII (March 23, 1946), 340-42.

Commager, Henry S., "How It All Looked to Mister Truman." *Reporter*, XIII (December 1, 1955), 42-45.

Congressional Digest, XXV (November, 1946), 257-88.

Congressional Quarterly Almanac, V (1949), 284.

Conn, Harry, "Housing: A Vanishing Vision." *New Republic*, CXXV (July 16, 1951), 12-14; (July 23, 1951), 10-13; (July 30, 1951), 12-13; (August 13, 1951), 15-16.

"Controls are Finished." *New Republic*, CXV (November 18, 1946), 659.

Dangerfield, George, "The Man Who Rode a Tiger." *Nation*, CLXXXII (March 17, 1956), 221-22.

Davis, Elmer, "Harry Truman and the Verdict of History." *Reporter,* VIII (February 3, 1953), 17-22.

Dean, John P., "Folklore and Taboos." *Nation,* CLXVI (May 15, 1948), 540-42.

——, "The Myths of Housing Reform." *American Sociological Review,* XIV (April, 1949), 281-88.

"A Decent Home for Every Family." *American City,* LIX (July, 1944), 91.

Degler, Carl N., "American Political Parties and the Rise of the City: An Interpretation." *Journal of American History,* LI (June, 1964), 41-59.

"The Dreary Deadlock of Public Housing and How to Break It." *Architectural Forum,* CVI (June, 1957), 139-41, 218, 222-32.

Dunham, H. Warren, and Grundstein, Nathan D., "The Impact of a Confusion of Social Objectives on Public Housing: A Preliminary Analysis." *Marriage and Family Living,* XXII (May, 1955), 103-12.

Eldersveld, Samuel J., "The Influence of Metropolitan Party Pluralities in Presidential Elections Since 1920: A Study of Twelve Key Cities." *The American Political Science Review,* XLIII (December, 1949), 1189-1206.

Ellender, Allen J., "What T-E-W Provides." *Nation,* CLXVI (May 15, 1948), 532.

"Equality in Housing." *New Republic,* CXXI (November 16, 1949), 8.

"Fight on Housing." *Business Week* (December 30, 1944), 21-22.

Foulkrod, Marjorie, "Case History of Housing." *Current History,* XV (September, 1949), 138-43.

Fuller, Helen, "Stalled in the Lobby." *New Republic,* CXVIII (March 1, 1948), 11-14.

Gray, George H., "Public Housing, a Function of Democracy." *Architectural Record,* XCIV (September, 1943), 52-53.

Greer, Guy, "Getting Ready for Federal Aid in Urban Redevelopment." *American City,* LVIII (May, 1943), 47-49.

——, "Housing: The Why of Planning." *Fortune,* XXX (November, 1944), 146-51.

Hansen, Alvin, "Urban Redevelopment." *Survey Graphic,* XXXIII (April, 1944), 204-5.

Harrington, Michael, "Slums, Old and New." *Commentary,* XXX (August, 1960), 118-24.

Headlines, Vols. X (1943) through XIX (1952).

Hill, John G., "Fifty Years of Social Action on the Housing Front." *Social Service Review,* XXII (June, 1948), 160-79.

Holden, Thomas S., "How Many Post-war Houses?" *Architectural Record,* XCIV (September, 1943), 50-51.

"The House Mess." *Fortune,* XXXV (January, 1947), 81-85.

"Housing Bill is Shelved." *American Federationist,* LIII (August, 1946), 15.

"Housing: Challenge and Failure." *New Republic,* CXVII (July 7, 1947), 19-21.

"Housing: Decisive Round Coming Up." *American Federationist,* LIII (May, 1946), 29.

"Housing, Not Lobbies." *New Republic,* CXIV (March 18, 1946), 367-68.

"Housing: Poor Hope." *New Republic,* CXV (December 9, 1946), 749.

"Housing Spurts and Sputters." *New Republic,* CXIV (June 3, 1946), 790-91.

"The Housing Victory." *Social Service Review,* XXIII (September, 1949), 379-80.

"Housing, War and Postwar." *Survey,* LXXIX (March, 1943), 84.

Hovde, B. J., "Housing for the Low Income Group." *Journal of Home Economics,* XXXVI (April, 1944), 208.

Huthmacher, J. Joseph, "Urban Liberalism and the Age of Reform." *Mississippi Valley Historical Review,* XLIX (October, 1962), 231-41.

Johnson, Lee F., "Fifteen Million Homes." *Nation,* CLXVI (May 15, 1948), 537.

———, "Housing: A 1950 Tragedy." *Survey,* LXXXVI (December, 1950), 551-55.

Klutznick, Philip N., "Better Homes for America." *Journal of Home Economics,* XXXVI (September, 1944), 421-22.

———, "A Decent Home for Every Family." *American City,* LIX (July, 1944), 91.

———, "Public Housing Charts Its Course." *Survey Graphic,* XXXIV (January, 1945), 15-18.

Koenig, Louis W., "Truman's Global Leadership." *Current History,* XXXIX (October, 1960), 225-29.

Lasch, Robert, "The Building Industry." *Nation,* CLXVI (May 15, 1948), 538-39.

Lasker, Loula D., "The Call of Our Cities." *Survey Graphic,* XXXIII (April, 1944), 197-98.

"Last Chance for Houses." *New Republic,* CXIX (May 24, 1948), 8.

Lee, R. Alton, "The Turnip Session of the Do-Nothing Congress: Presidential Campaign Strategy." *The Southwestern Social Science Quarterly,"* XLIV (December, 1963), 256-67.

Life, XIX (December 17, 1945), 27-36.

Lubove, Roy, "Homes and 'A Few Well Placed Fruit Trees': An Object Lesson in Federal Housing." *Social Research,* XXVII (Winter, 1960), 469-86.

———, "New Cities for Old: The Urban Reconstruction Program of the 1930's." *Social Studies,* LIII (November, 1962), 203-13.

Lynd, Staughton, "Urban Renewal—For Whom?" *Commentary*, XXXI (January, 1961), 34-46.

Martin, Ralph G., "Homes for Veterans." *New Republic*, CXIII (December 10, 1945), 791-93.

Mercer, Max, "That Postwar Dream House." *Antioch Review*, III (December, 1943), 558-73.

Merriam, Charles E., "The National Resources Planning Board: A Chapter in American Planning Experience." *American Political Science Review*, XXXVIII (December, 1944), 1075-88.

"Mr. Wyatt Builds His Castle." *Fortune*, XXXIV (July, 1946), 3.

"Mr. Wyatt's Housing Shortage." *Fortune*, XXXIII (April, 1946), 105-13.

Monson, Donald and Astrid, "Ideas from Sweden." *American City*, LXIV (March, 1949), 84-86; (April, 1949), 110-11; (May, 1949), 140-42.

Moore, Ruth, "Building Tomorrow's Slums." *New Republic*, CXVI (January 6, 1947), 17-20.

Morgan, H. Wayne, "History and the Presidency: Harry S. Truman." *Phylon Quarterly*, XIX (July, 1958), 162-70.

Nation, CLXIII (November 16, 1946), 541.

Neustadt, Richard E., "Congress and the Fair Deal; A Legislative Balance Sheet." *Public Policy*, V (1954), 351-81.

Newsweek, XXVII (January 21, 1946), 37; (February 18, 1946), 37; (April 8, 1946), 66; (September 21, 1946), 25; XXXIII (September 10, 1951), 80.

"New York's Housing Week." *American City*, LIX (June, 1944), 95-97.

Patterson, Chat, "Housing." *Antioch Review*, VIII (December, 1948), 393-98.

———, "Veterans Want Action." *Nation*, CLXVI (May 15, 1948), 546-48.

"Planning and Politics." *Nation*, CLVI (March 20, 1943), 405-7.

Podhoretz, Norman, "Truman and the Idea of the Common Man." *Commentary*, XXI (May, 1956), 469-74.

"The Promise of the Shortage." *Fortune*, XXXIII (April, 1946), 101-3.

"Public Housing Gets a Drubbing." *Business Week* (May 27, 1950), 26.

"Public Housing in the Doldrums." *New Republic*, CX (May 1, 1944), 595-96.

Putney, Bryant, "Obituary for Veterans' Housing." *Nation*, CLXIII (December 21, 1946), 722-23.

Robbins, Ira S., "Housing Goals and Achievements in the United States." *American Journal of Economics and Sociology*, XV (April, 1956), 285-92.

———, "Slums Are Like Treadmills." *Survey Graphic*, XXXIII (April, 1944), 207.

Rosenman, Dorothy, "A Truce Upon Your Housing." *Survey Graphic*, XXXIII (January, 1944), 20-22.
Sancton, Thomas, "Housing and Segregation." *Nation*, CLXVIII (April, 1949), 490-91.
Schmidtlein, Eugene F., "Truman's First Senatorial Election." *Missouri Historical Review*, LVII (January, 1963), 128-55.
Seligman, Daniel, "The Enduring Slums." *Fortune*, LVI (December, 1957), 144-48, 214-24.
"Shambles." *New Republic*, CXV (December 16, 1946), 791-92.
"The Shape of Things." *Nation*, CLXIII (November 16, 1946), 541.
Shiskin, Boris, "Homes for the Brave." *American Federationist*, LVII (March, 1946), 8-11.
Smith, Bernard B., "Those Post-war Houses?" *Harper's*, CLXXXVII (July, 1943), 108-14.
"Sold Out: No Houses." *New Republic*, CXIX (September 27, 1948), 12-13.
Sparkes, Boydon, "Can the Cities Come Back?" *Saturday Evening Post*, CCXVII (November 4, 1944), 28-29, 42, 44.
"Start in Housing." *New Republic*, CXX (May 2, 1949), 6-7.
Steinberg, Alfred, "FHA—Profits Before Housing." *Nation*, CLXVIII (January 1, 1949), 11-13.
Stone, I. F., "Planning and Politics." *Nation*, CLVI (March 20, 1943), 405-7.
———, "Some News to Cheer." *Nation*, CLXII (February 16, 1946), 186-87.
Straus, Nathan, "A Business Man's Prescription." *Nation*, CLXVI (May 15, 1948), 544-45.
"T-E-W—Now or Never." *Nation*, CLXVI (May 15, 1948), 519.
Thomas, R. J., "Labor Views." *Survey Graphic*, XXXIII (April, 1944), 212.
Time, XLVI (October 22, 1945), 21; XLVII (April 8, 1946), 22-23; XLVIII (November 25, 1946), 89; (December 9, 1946), 24; (December 24, 1946), 22-24.
Tough, Rosiland, "What's Behind Housing?" *Social Service Review*, XXIII (March, 1949), 25-38.
Truman, Harry S, "A Plan for the Regional Developments of To-morrow." *Civil Engineering*, XIV (November, 1944), 465.
U.S. News & World Report, XX (February 8, 1946), 65-66; (February 15, 1946), 66-67; (May 8, 1946), 30-31; XXI (October 18, 1946), 19; (October 25, 1946), 26.
"Veterans' Non-Housing." *New Republic*, CXVI (January 6, 1947), 12.
Wallace, Henry, "Conspiracy Against Housing." *New Republic*, CXVIII (March 1, 1948), 10.
"Where We Stand Today in Housing." *American City*, LX (February, 1945), 70.

Index

Long, Huey, 34-35

Los Angeles, California, 40

Louisiana, 35

Low-income families: need for housing discussed, x, 37, 70. *See also* Public housing

Lubell, Samuel: interpretation of Truman Administration, 135

Lustron Company: and VEHP, 52-54; and McCarthy, 71; and Wyatt's resignation, 57

McCarthy, Joseph R.: and the Joint Committee on Housing, 68-72; and "Individual Views," 70; and Special Session of Congress, 93-94; mention of, 117

McCarthy Housing Bill, 93-95

McClellan, John, 113

McCormack, John, 49, 122

McDonnell, Timothy, 8

Madison, Wisconsin, 96

Maenner, T. H.: and public housing, 109-10

Martin, Joe: and Message on Reconversion, 32-33; and public housing, 108; mention of, 79, 92, 109

Maybank, Burnet: and housing legislation, 105; mention of, 132

Memoirs: by Harry S Truman, 89

Mental illness: relationship to poor housing, x

Merrion, Joseph E.: and public housing, 20

Message on Reconversion, 31-32, 54, 56, 72

Middle-income housing bill: defeat in Congress, 117-21; mention of, 27

Monroney, Mike: quoted on Republican party and housing legislation, 81

Murphy, Charles S.: and Special Session of Congress, 84

National Association for Advancement of Colored People: and FHA, 124-25

National Association of Home Builders, 15, 60, 62, 109, 127

National Association of Real Estate Boards: convention opposition to Wagner-Ellender-Taft bill, 38; mention of, 15, 109. *See also* Real estate lobby; Nelson, Herbert U.

National Committee on Housing, 15

National health insurance, 102

National Housing Act of 1934, 8

National Housing Agency: Wyatt appointed administrator, 44; replaced by HHFA; mention of, 10, 25, 27, 61

National Housing Association, 4-5, 15

National housing policy: and Joint Committee on Housing, 70; and Truman, 114-15, 142; mention of, 32, 33, 117

National Industrial Recovery Act: and public housing, 8; mention of, 2, 36, 48

National Labor Relations Act, 2, 36

National Mortgage Company, 118

National Public Housing Conference: and strengths of, 15; and weaknesses of, 128-29

National Resources Planning Board: congressional opposition to, 23-25; and 1944 Economic Bill of Rights, 25; *Report*, 23, 32. *See also* Conservative coalition

National Securities Resources Board, 123

Negroes: and housing discrimination, 35, 116; impact of northern migration of, 123-24; and FHA, 124-25; and public housing, 107-8

Nelson, Herbert U.: opposition to public housing, 17; director of Realtors' Washington Committee, 22; mention of, 119. *See also* Real estate lobby

Neustadt, Richard, 130

New Deal: and Truman, ix, 31; and housing reform, ix, 7-9; and urban liberalism, 2-3; and United States Housing Act of